DARK KniGHTs & HOLY FOOLS

DARK KNIGHTS & HOLY FOOLS

ORION

First published in Great Britain by
The Orion Publishing Group
5 Upper St Martin's Lane
London WC2H 9EA

A CIP catalogue for this book is available from the British Library.

ISBN 0-75281-827-9 Hardback

ISBN 0-75281-851-1 Paperback

Colour Origination by Colourwise Ltd, Sussex, England.

Printed in Italy.

DEDICATION:

For Lucy, Jessie and the Player to be Named Later,
due to arrive around the same time as this book.
(Bob McCabe)

WHEN BOB APPROACHED ME about this book I was in the middle of making *Fear and Loathing In Las Vegas*. As I continued with that movie, it started to become clear to me that it was in many ways a culmination of many things for me, maybe even a natural end to one stage of my work. So now seemed like a good time to look back at what we've been doing all these years. One of the things both Bob and myself wanted to highlight was the visual aspect of all the movies – you can write about them all you want but these movies are basically there to be seen. In light of this, I opened up my own archive for this book, allowing many sketches, storyboards and photos to be used for the very first time.

Terry Gilliam

Dark Knights and Holy Fools, a sketch by Terry Gilliam, January 1999

Contents

ACKNOWLEDGMENTS

The Age of Unreasonable Deadlines.

THERE IS A WONDERFUL BRITISH PHRASE. It may not even be British; it may just be English, but anyway, it's 'arse-ways round'. It's probably a distant cousin of 'putting the cart before the horse', but it works. I was reminded of it halfway through writing this book. It was only deep in the middle of what, at that point, seemed like a Herculean task that I actually realised *why* I wanted to write the book in the first place (of course I should have known that up front – arse-ways round). As someone who earns their living from watching, talking and writing about movies, there are two questions you are always asked (generally at dinner parties, when the person next to you has realised you have nothing interesting to say and they are looking for a fall-back). Those questions are: 'What's good on at the moment?' the real sign that the dinner party is not going well, and 'Who's your favourite actor/actress/director?' (not as easy as you'd think to answer that one). If you earn your living watching movies, sooner or later every-one lets you down. Steve Martin did *Bilko*; Bill Murray did that thing with the elephant; Woody slept with Soon-Yi – it happens. And that was when it occurred to me: Terry Gilliam has *never* let me down. He has, instead, presented me with some of the most remarkable experiences I have ever had in a dark-ened room. He has dazzled me with visions beyond my wildest imaginings, and produced a body of work that strikes me not only as one of the most unique and fiercely intelligent in modern cinema, but also one of the most highly personal. Robin Williams says that 'he makes movies that people, I think, feel are made at night, and after they're asleep.' He knows a thing or two, that Robin Williams.

When I set out to write this book, I wanted it to capture a moment in a career that has still got a long way to go. Terry is a master at equipping all of his movies with clever and witty soundbites, such as 'the other side of now' and 'a cinematic enema for the '90s.' What I wanted to do was to take Terry's very considerable body of work and get him to look back on it as such – see how it connects, chart how it develops, find out how and where it relates. I also wanted to illustrate the book with as many unseen pictures, sketches and paintings as I could find, and for this he very kindly gave me full access to his considerable archive, a veritable Aladdin's treasure cave located somewhere in North London.

There were several things I promised myself I would not do as well. I did not want to dwell on Python because, beside the fact that it been covered exhaustively elsewhere, I felt that Python was by now a relatively small part of Gilliam's career. I also did not want to overemphasize *Brazil* and *The Adventures of Baron Munchausen*, as the stories behind those movies have already been captured brilliantly in Jack Mathews' *The Battle of Brazil* and Andrew Yule's *Losing the Light*. But as we progressed, I found that Gilliam was the Python whose visuals not only shaped the show, but who also seems to have said the least about the whole experience over the years. Similarly, *Brazil* and *Munchausen* and the stories of their making have, for better or worse, helped define cinema as we know it – and they're damn good stories.

The interviews herein were conducted during the editing, and up to shortly after the release, of *Fear and Loathing in Las Vegas*. As that film evolved, an opportune moment seemed to arise to get Gilliam to look back on his work. His American films, *The Fisher King*, *Twelve Monkeys* and *Fear and Loathing*, were now beginning to emerge as a trilogy, much as his British trio of *Time Bandits*, *Brazil* and *Munchausen* did. Between the two sets of three, there seemed to be an amazing journey, that of a man who had left one country for another, who had valiantly defended fantasy above all else, had been praised and pilloried in

October 1998. Around bedtime.

equal measure for doing so, and who had begun to return to his homeland and to explore the reality there. The fantasy, the magic, was still there but now it wasn't an escape; it was a companion. *Fear and Loathing in Las Vegas* feels like the end of something, a good time to look at what has gone before. At this stage, I have no idea what Terry Gilliam will do next. Terry Gilliam has no idea what he will do next. There is only one certainty – whatever it turns out to be, we would all be wise to follow the tag line on the *Fear and Loathing* poster: 'Buy the ticket. Take the ride.'

There are, inevitably, a vast amount of people to thank. I am deeply indebted to Terry's wife, Maggie Weston, who does an amazing job of effortlessly concealing all the ducts and working mechanisms of *chez* Gilliam, not an easy task I am sure. Many thanks to Robin Williams, who gave up his lunch break during the hectic filming of *Patch Adams* to regale me with extremely amusing and insightful tales of Terry. Similarly, I must thank Michael Palin and Richard LaGravenese for taking time out of their busy schedules, and for their informative insights. Charles McKeown very kindly welcomed me into his home, where he filled in a number of gaps in the *Brazil* and *Munchausen* stories. Tony Grisoni also invited me into his home, although there was no home there at the time so we repaired to the local pub. He buys a good pint, and he has my eternal gratitude for doing so. Thanks are also due to Michael Kamen, Johnny Depp, Benicio Del Toro, Kent Houston of Peerless Camera and Roanne Moore of the *Fear and Loathing* office for all her help in arranging interviews during the early stages of this book.

A special thank you to Dr Mark Kermode, who was a great help as always, and to Alan Jones for his exclusive photos from the Alan Jones Collection and, well, just for being Alan Jones. For friendship and spare change, I am eternally indebted (in every sense of the word) to the likes of Rob Churchill, Paul Gillion, Michael Samuels and countless others.

Additionally, many thanks to the staff at both *Empire* and *Sight and Sound* and, as always, to the staff at the British Film Industry library – where would we be without their stuff?

Love and thanks, as always, to Mary McCabe.

Without Mal Peachey and John Conway there would be no book (too Tom Hanks, do you think?) – they are noble men in a seamy world. Finally, as ever, love, eternal gratitude and even more love to Lucy Merritt and the wonderfully compact Jessie McCabe, who make writing a book longer, but a hell of a lot more fun.

Oh, and finally, finally, I owe a great debt of gratitude to Terry Gilliam, who not only welcomed me into his home, made me vast amounts of tea, gave up countless hours answering, let's face it, some pretty dumb questions, and then let me rummage through just about everything he owned. It was done with good grace, warmth and a bloody good laugh. (You see, I should have thanked him first – arse-ways round.)

BOB McCABE
OCTOBER 1998

(The author would like to point out that this book was written the old-fashioned way. At no point was the internet used, abused, involved or invoked. Good night. Safe dreams.)

Two-legged portrait of
Teddy Roosevelt

Prologue

TERRENCE VANCE GILLIAM was born on 22 November 1940, into the small rural community of Medicine Lake, Minnesota, a few miles west of Minneapolis. For a child where boyhood games (and, later, adult visions) prominently featured medieval knights, his father added the glamorous touch of having served in the last mounted unit of the U.S. Cavalry. Subsequently, his father, James Hall Gilliam, helped build the Alaskan highway, which kept him away from his family for some considerable time, as did his next job as a travelling salesman for Folger's coffee.

Eventually, the family settled down in Medicine Lake where Gilliam's father worked as a carpenter. The birth of a daughter followed and then another son arrived, almost a decade after the first, who would later become a high-ranking detective in the Los Angeles Police Department.

With its population of largely Scandinavian descent, the future filmmaker would later describe Medicine Lake as '*Fargo* country,' in reference to the Coen brothers' movie. It was a dirt road town, and the Gilliams' house stood a mere couple of blocks from the nearby lake, with a swamp across the way and a big woods beyond. 'I think it was influential in the sense that I was born in the country,' Gilliam later recalled. 'I'm a country boy basically. It was a Tom Sawyer–Huckleberry Finn existence. What I remember most is playing in the swamp amongst cut trees, logs and moss-covered caves, which were great hidey holes.'

In summer, the swamp steamed; in winter the snow drifts brought forty degree-below winds. His Medicine Lake toilet was to play at least a small part in his development. Gilliam later commented, 'I'm fascinated with toilets. Not just things that bring stuff to us, but things that take away as well.' He also explained, 'We had an outdoor toilet for years, but I have no sense memory of what it was like in the winter, when it was forty degrees below zero, to go out for a dump in the "biffy" – as they were called – in the back garden. That must have been painful, but I don't remember it. But I do remember that when we finally got an indoor toilet, we dismantled the biffy and I used the wood to build myself a three-storey high tree house.'

It was in the tree house that he would read voraciously; dog books at first – '*Lassie* and all these Scottish books about highland dogs. They were about loyalty, master and servant relationships – like fairy tales in a sense.' Grander stories came in the form of comic books, most notably the illustrated classics series that fed the young Gilliam's imagination with *Moby Dick, Treasure Island* and *Ivanhoe*. Soon Terry was cutting down tree branches and making them into swords, using five-gallon ice-cream containers as improvised helmets, 'and we'd make these great big wooden shields and I'd paint them, and then we'd go and bash each other senseless.'

A salute to the mothers of America

Gilliam could always draw. He has no memory of any time when it was not part of his life. He was quick, however, to discover that he had a distinct ability for it and that this could indeed have its own rewards. A school field trip to the local zoo was the impetus. The students were supposed to draw an animal from memory when they returned. 'I cheated,' relates Gilliam. 'I had a book in my lap with a picture of a bear, so I drew this really good picture of a bear and I got a box of crayons as my reward. So my art career began by cheating, which I think I've done ever since.

'I just started drawing cartoons. I never drew "art". I was drawing Martians, but they were Martians that looked like vacuum cleaners. I'd started turning household appliances into extra-terrestrials. And there were always those big books *How to Draw Cartoons* and that's where I learned to draw cartoons. I did think it was something I could do. And I could always entertain people with it. I could always surprise people. With cartoons you get immediate feedback. You write something and it's never that immediate. It's like showing off all the time. And it was nice to have people say "Aren't you talented? Clever boy".'

There were other influences. A magic set his father had bought him nurtured his ideas of illusion, learning how to manipulate things to achieve your own aim. The travelling circuses and sideshows that passed through Medicine Lake also fuelled Gilliam's imagination, offering him a world full of freakish anomalies, from bearded ladies to dwarves. And, of course, there was radio. Gilliam devoured the fairy tales of *Let's Pretend*, the action adventure of *The Green Hornet*, the crime dramas of *The FBI at Peace and War* and *The Shadow*. 'I think radio developed my visual sense, because I'd invent it all. I've always thought you can create more atmosphere with radio than with film or with any other form because it's all imagination on the listener's part.'

Some friends up the road from the Gilliams eventually brought television to Medicine Lake. Gilliam's first experience of the medium came in the form of comedian Ernie Kovacs. Hailing from Philadelphia, Kovacs appeared in two shows during the early 1950s – *Ernie in Kovacsland* and *The Ernie Kovacs Show*, both of which brought a unique seam of visual comedy to American network television. Kovacs' style blended slapstick with a then unprecedented level of surrealism, taking humour to unexpected places and levels his contemporaries never reached. Both Chevy Chase and the late Andy Kaufman cited him as a major influence, and his style had a clear, albeit indirect, influence on the stream of consciousness approach the Pythons took to the sketch-show format. 'It was the first time I'd bumped into surrealism and surrealistic comedy,' says Gilliam. 'He [Kovacs] even did his own ads, because Dutch Master Cigars used to sponsor his show. There was one great gag – two gunfighters are having a big shoot-out and one of them falls down dead and the other one goes up to the bar, lights a cigar and a thousand holes of smoke come out of him.'

In 1951, the Gilliam clan moved west to California. 'Moving out to L.A. I thought it was going to be cowboys and Indians. We were going out to the Wild West in my imagination because California was what I'd seen in the movies, all those Westerns.' The reality of the expected 'wilds' of Panorama City was closer to the colour co-ordinated tract housing of Tim Burton's *Edward Scissorhands*. 'About three years before we got there it was all orange groves and sheep farms. Like in *Chinatown* when he goes out to the valley – this was that valley. Henry Kaiser of Kaiser Aluminum tore it all down and they built this huge tract there, and I grew up in that kind of new suburbia.'

This new suburbia was not without its delights, however. First and foremost there were the movies, where Gilliam took his love of comic strips and began to transfer it to an understanding of animation. Walt Disney, needless to say, helped. 'I remember *Snow White, Pinocchio*, which were beautiful because the craftsmanship was so wonderful, the detail, the background colours. Those were the ones I loved. It's funny because seeing things like [shorts by] Tex Avery and Chuck Jones weren't the same. They were funnier and they were zippier and I loved them, but I never knew who Chuck Jones or Tex Avery were. Disney was the only name you knew if you were talking about animation. I remember, years ago, seeing *Pinocchio* again and recognising that it's a really short, tight little film and yet it opens up your imagination. I think *Pinocchio* is probably my favourite because everything is in there. *Snow White* is also wonderful, particularly the dwarves. For better or worse, what Disney always did with Grimms' fairy tales, or any fairy tales, was fill them with really good characters to carry you through the stuff.'

From early childhood, fairy tales had been a staple part of Gilliam's literary diet and they would remain a huge influence on his later work, particularly his early films as director, which either adopted the classic fairy tale structure (*Jabberwocky*), played around with their general mythology (*Time Bandits*) or defended their very right to exist in a rational world (*The Adventures of Baron Munchausen*). 'Fairy tales should confront your fears,' Gilliam argues. 'I remember years ago a book had snuck into the house and it was this bowdlerised version of *Little Red Riding Hood* – the wolf doesn't actually eat grandma, she hides in the closet, and the woodsman is daddy who comes and chases the wolf away. It was pathetic because it's not dealing with any of the fears. I remember there was a screening of *Munchausen* at the ICA in London, for kids, and this woman afterwards was really angry with me because the figure of death was frightening to her child. But *that's* the point of it. I think the mother is going to have more nightmares than the little girl. What I keep finding is that the kids take it much more easily than the adults. For me, with kids and fairy tales, I say scare the shit out of the little bastards because then they'll get used to it and then they can handle it when life comes up with something scary.'

Movies opened doorways to other worlds far removed from suburbia and fostered Gilliam's love of history. 'I didn't read more than anybody else. I did read a lot, but it was always casual, as it came easy. So it was movies, *Ivanhoe* and all that stuff. I was always fascinated with it. And I remember when Disneyland was built. I was actually back East with my grandparents and I was just fascinated by the idea of Disneyland and a castle. The first chance I had to see a castle. And then years later I came to Europe and saw real castles. I'm never sure which was better. The Middle Ages always interested me. It's a simple society, the hierarchy is very clear. And Westerns and knights, they're very similar things. You have a very clear hierarchy, a very clear structure and so you can play within that. There's nothing complex about it to a childish mind, which is just great. It still continues to be great.'

Coming from such a relatively closed community in the American Midwest of the 1940s, organised religion – in this case Presbyterianism – exerted a strong influence over the Gilliam family, and moving out to California did not alter that. Terry became leader of the church youth

An early 20th century copy of the Baron's tales

group and later attended Occidental College on a Presbyterian scholarship. At one point, Gilliam planned to devote his life to the church, with thoughts of becoming a missionary. 'There were two good things about that,' Gilliam now recollects. 'First the sense of community, which I do actually miss, and secondly, the Bible stories are fantastic, really good tales. Our kids [he is now the father of three] have been raised with no religion as such, and I keep thinking it's kind of a pity because those tales are extraordinarily powerful and they don't know them. Maybe I've deprived them.'

Away from the church, Gilliam was discovering more secular influences, once again in the form of the circus sideshows he had visited back in Medicine Lake. When the circus stopped at Panorama City, twelve-year-old Gilliam got a job for the day raising the freak show tent. 'That was the thing that really stuck with me about that day, wandering around before the crowds came and all the freaks, doing ordinary things, dressed ordinarily, before they got into costume and became the "most deformed person on the planet", or whatever, and that always stuck with me. It's a fascination with people who are unique or different and, at the same time, the normalcy of the whole thing.' During Monty Python, intimidated by the rest of the team's performing abilities, Gilliam would tellingly opt to play the 'freaks or grotesques'.

Gilliam attended Birmingham High School, where he was not only a straight 'A' student, but a pole vaulting letterman, president of the student body, class valedictorian and king of the senior prom. His image was that of a crew-cut jock. His perfect high school record was all set to be duplicated at Occidental College. With 1200 to 1500 students, Occidental was a relatively small campus with a strong reputation and a student body largely made up of the offspring of prominent, wealthy families. Gilliam was there on a scholarship but instantly felt at home: 'It was like being in this safe, secure world where everybody's intelligent, and you can start the jokes at a certain level.'

Gilliam pledged the Sigma Alpha Epsilon fraternity where practical jokes played a big part in campus life. It wasn't unusual here for a student to find his room stuffed to bursting with rolled up newspaper, or to unlock his front door only to have it shoot across the room because its hinges had been removed and his bed was tied to it and now dangling from his dorm window. On one memorable occasion, a car was taken apart, reassembled and left running in another student bedroom.

He began life at Occidental majoring in physics, but after a few weeks decided to follow his natural impulses and switched to art. However, a failure to communicate with the art history teacher led him to change his major to political science, a course that allowed Gilliam to dip into a variety of subjects, ranging from Oriental philosophy to drama.

Having abandoned his plans to become a missionary, Gilliam now sought a way to combine his natural artistic talents with a sensible profession and decided on architecture. One summer he took a job at a leading local architecture firm and found himself, not for the last time in his career, facing the demon that is compromise. 'I thought it was disgusting,' Gilliam recounts. 'This firm was a very successful one in L.A. but they were very good at bending over backwards to meet the demands of the clients rather than fighting for good designs. That's probably why they were successful.'

More and more of Gilliam's time as a student was being consumed by extracurricular activities. As before, his natural ability at cartooning was proving useful. 'We used to get rolls of butcher paper and every night we'd make huge posters and signs and in the morning people would come down from the dorms and see all this stuff on the walls of the canteen. It had been started before, but myself and a couple of other people, who were also cartoonists, did it non-stop and we loved it, so we became a kind of entertainment for everybody.'

By far the most significant of these pastimes was Gilliam's involvement in the college magazine during his senior year. Originally a three-times-a-year literary magazine, Gilliam and friends took it over, renamed it *Fang* and packed it with humour and cartoons, which were heavily influenced by Harvey Kurtzman's original *Mad* comics. *Mad* had long been a Gilliam favourite, with such great *Mad* alumni as Wally Wood and Jack Davis proving a strong influence on his emerging cartoon style. When Kurtzman quit *Mad*, taking his team of cartoonists with him, he eventually launched America's first national humour magazine, *Help!*. Gloria Steinem was Kurtzman's first assistant editor on it. Charles Alverson, who replaced Steinem, later co-scripted *Jabberwocky* and the first draft of *Brazil* with Gilliam. Greatly encouraged by his work on *Fang*, Gilliam sent copies of the magazine to Kurtzman in New York, who replied praising the magazine, thus bolstering Gilliam's confidence.

Gilliam worked his way through college with a number of jobs, including a stint on the local Chevrolet assembly line. After graduation, as his college clique went their separate ways, Gilliam was faced with uncertainty about his future. As a stop-gap he took a job at a children's theatre and summer camp, making sets, painting himself green and 'playing the ogre'.

Gilliam's stint at the summer camp saw him counselling the children of such celebrities as Danny Kaye, Hedy Lamarr and Burt Lancaster. It also saw him encountering his first example of production problems. As drama coach at the camp, Gilliam was in charge of the end-of-summer production. He had chosen to stage *Alice in Wonderland*, but soon realised the production was spiralling out of control. 'The big thing was parents' weekend,' he recalls of this formative moment. 'I had this all-star cast, and maybe a week before the event I said "We're not doing it. It's a disaster. Nothing is ready." It was a complete fuck up. We'd taken on too much, it was so disorganised. And I pulled the plug on it and the centrepiece of the parents' weekend was not there.'

This haunting disaster aside, Gilliam found himself, via the summer camp, around the Beverly Hills elite and tantalisingly close to the movie business, and recognised it was something of which he wanted to be a part. 'But I didn't know how you got to make films,' Gilliam says. 'I was really close to the whole thing but frustrated at not knowing how. I didn't want to work my way up through the business. I didn't want to be a tea boy. I'd made this pact with myself never to work just for the money and only do work I had some control over. I made these rules for myself and I stuck by them.' This declaration of intent was given added grist when, over that summer, Gilliam read *Act One*, the autobiography of playwright Moss Hart. 'Moss Hart was a cocky lad coming down to New York and meeting up with George Kaufman and then, suddenly, they're Kaufman and Hart, writing all these great plays. So I thought, "I've got to go to New York".'

The only person he even vaguely knew in New York was *Help!* editor Harvey Kurtzman, so he wrote to him. 'And he wrote me a letter back saying "don't bother, there's nothing here for you, kid."

But I went to New York anyway because I didn't have any other plans. I met Harvey in the Algonquin Hotel. Kurtzman had taken a suite upstairs and stuffed all his cartoonists in there and they were working on this thing. So I went up there and the door opens and there are all my heroes in this room. Harvey turns up a bit later and it turns out that Chuck Alverson, the assistant editor on the magazine, was quitting and they needed somebody to take over his job, so I walked right into it. I was thinking "this isn't supposed to happen like this," but it happened to Moss Hart and then it happened to me.'

Gilliam started working on *Help!* magazine in 1962 and stayed until the magazine folded in 1965. 'Working for *Help!* I was being paid two dollars less than I would have been paid on the dole,' says Gilliam, 'but I was doing great work and having a great time.'

The magazine was essentially a two-man operation – Kurtzman and Gilliam – but it served as a vehicle for some of the finest artists and humorists of its day, including Gilbert Shelton, Jay Lynch and Robert Crumb. It allowed Gilliam to explore the rich delights of New York, amongst them film night school, at which he only lasted a month before quitting. 'I then got a job in a studio that did stop-motion animation, dancing cigarette packets and things. I got a job there for free. The guy said, "We've got no money." I said, "Let me just work, I'll sweep up, whatever." I was in a real place with real cameras and real lights, which was far better than the film school.'

Gilliam's work on *Help!* was also aiding his understanding of film. One of his main functions was to produce the magazine's distinctive *fumetti* – photo comic strips that essentially played like a movie storyboard, with Gilliam often writing, casting and photographing them himself. 'That's where I met lots of people, particularly Henry Jaglom and Jim Hampton, who went on to become the bugler in the TV series *F Troop*. I had a friend, Judy Henske, a folk singer, who asked if she could bring her boyfriend, who turned out to be Woody Allen, so Woody Allen is in one of our strips.' He played Mister Big, a boater-wearing gangster in a Gilliam gangster parody. But the most significant person Gilliam was to meet via these *fumetti*, however, was a young British comedy actor named John Cleese.

The British satirical revue *Beyond the Fringe*, featuring Peter Cook, Dudley Moore, Jonathan Miller and Alan Bennett, had recently added Broadway to its list of triumphs. Another revue, this time by the Cambridge Footlights and titled *Cambridge Circus*, followed hot on its heels. Unlike its predecessor, *Cambridge Circus* met with a mixed response and closed on Broadway after only twenty three performances. It did, however, find another life in the infinitely more suitable surroundings of the Square East Theater down in Greenwich Village, where it enjoyed a successful run. It was here that Terry Gilliam saw the show.

'They were brilliant,' he recalled. 'There was Graham (Chapman) and John, Bill Oddie, David Hatch and Tim Brooke-Taylor. I saw the show and of course John stood out, as always, and I asked him if he'd be in one of these *fumetti* and that's how we became friends.' Cleese appeared in a strip entitled 'Christopher's Punctured Romance' as a husband beset with a terrible case of ennui, who

finds love and more than a little implied sexual satisfaction with his seven-year-old's Barbie doll.

Gilliam was keen to move beyond these frame-by-frame still stories into twenty four frames per second action. To this end he bought a 16mm Bolex camera and a tape recorder and decided to try to unlock the secret of making movies. 'There were three of us living in this flat and on weekends we'd write a little movie and we'd go out and shoot it, just to do this stuff and to play at the business of making movies.' The experience also led to his first efforts at animating: 'We were always stealing film from trash cans and drawing on it. We'd animate right on the clear film. So we were constantly beginning to make films. We never finished anything. We'd get it halfway there, but nothing was ever put together properly. It was more for the fun of doing it.'

During his three-year stint on the magazine, *Help!* was as close as American magazine humour got to satire or taking an anti-establishment stance. Its assistant editor, meanwhile, was also serving his time in the National Guard. Joining the National Guard was Gilliam's way of avoiding the draft for Vietnam, but it nonetheless entailed a lengthy period of basic training across the river from New York, at Fort Dix in New Jersey.

'Again the cartooning came in useful,' Gilliam remembers. 'At the end of boot camp when everybody was out on their belly in the mud, under machine gun fire and barbed wire, I was sitting in the barracks drawing portraits. During the last part of basic training, after the boot camp part, I was on the post newspaper doing cartoons there, and again I could stretch it out, doing one cartoon a week. What you learn in the army is to malinger, which I hate. I hated being in the army. It was madness. The war was getting uglier and all these guys were wanting to go and serve their country. They didn't really want to serve their country, they just wanted to have a good bash. They found it exciting. And at the same time I'm drawing anti-government, anti-war cartoons.'

By 1965, *Help!* was on its last legs and Gilliam decided to take six months out to hitchhike round Europe. 'I fell in love with Europe. It was that sudden thing of getting out of the cocoon of America and American thinking. I would be travelling somewhere and somebody would start giving me trouble for being an American and the war and stuff, and I'd get really angry and start defending America. It was frightening to find myself sounding like this terrible right-winger. It was like, "I can criticise but nobody else can." Going to Europe and just seeing those worlds and cultures really opened my eyes. There were real castles too.' Having grown up dreaming of the heraldry of medieval knights, the castles made a real impression, so much so that years later Gilliam bought one of his own in Italy. 'I was a huge Anglophile when it came to film,' Gilliam continues. 'I loved *The Goon Shows*, all the Ealing comedies and English films in general. I remember when I first came to London spending all my time trying to find the locations used in *Blow Up*.'

On a subsequent visit to England, Gilliam went to Hampton Court and then walked to nearby Shepperton Studios. He tried to bluff his way onto the backlot but was refused entry by the guards on the gate. Not one to be rebuffed easily, Gilliam walked round the corner, scaled the wall and

proceeded to make Shepperton his own for the day. 'I walked around the whole studio on my own,' he remembers, 'through the set of *Oliver*, everywhere. I walked into editing rooms and all the doors were unlocked; it was my studio. Then I walked out the front gate, past the guards. Years later I made *Jabberwocky* there.'

His brief trip to Shepperton fuelled Gilliam's lust for film, but still cartooning seemed to be the way to earn a living. 'Films were in my mind the whole time and I wanted to make them, but I couldn't see how you did it. So I did the cartoons because they were more immediate and I could sell them. It was a case of waiting, of trying to find a way of getting to make films without having to go through the tedious business of being a tea boy.'

Finding himself short of cash, Gilliam stopped off at *Pilote* magazine in Paris and did some work for Rene Goscinny, the creator of *Asterix the Gaul*. He was also filing some material back to *Esquire* magazine in the States. A visit to Britain's premiere satire magazine, *Private Eye*, however, was less successful. 'I showed them my cartoons and nobody was interested,' he laughs. 'The whole front cover of *Private Eye* with the speech balloons was taken from *Help!* magazine. *Help!* did it first. So I sort of went as a representative of *Help!* [and] I got short shrift.'

Gilliam's money ran out in Turkey. He managed to make it back to Paris to earn his fare home by working at *Pilote*. Then it was back to New York and Harvey Kurtzman's attic. After a few weeks there, working as a freelance illustrator for children's books, Gilliam headed out West and back to Los Angeles. Here he hooked up with writer Joel Siegel (now a leading movie critic on American television) and had a book, *The Cocktail Party*, published, with drawings by Gilliam and text by Siegel.

Siegel soon found himself working for a leading advertising agency and invited Terry to join him. 'I was the resident long-hair,' Gilliam remembers. 'I was the groovy guy, I guess, and I got a job as a copywriter and art director so I got to do a whole campaign myself. I lasted eleven months there and hated it.'

The West Coast was an interesting place to be at this time, with what would become known as the 'Summer of Love' just around the corner. 'I always compare it with Eden before Adam named the animals. Things were just happening. I was living in Laurel Canyon and there'd be a beautiful girl out there in her shift dancing in the dew. Life was kinda extraordinary. Then it all started being encroached upon by Madison Avenue. They grabbed onto it really quick and started incorporating everything that was happening into ads, which I thought really irritating.'

However, this self-styled Eden was rapidly being visited by more than one serpent. Vietnam was worsening, with President Lyndon Johnson increasing America's involvement on an almost daily basis. Despite the hippie ideology of peace and love, racism was exploding into violence in the inner cities, leading to the infamous Watts riots. It was something that Gilliam was to experience first-hand and which proved the final catalyst in his decision to leave his home country.

Gilliam was on his way to a party with his then girlfriend Glenys Roberts, a reporter for the

London *Evening Standard*, when they heard that police action in nearby Century City had sparked a riot. Roberts went to cover the action and Gilliam went with her. 'There were cops everywhere and it was all going fine until the cops went berserk and we ended up in the middle of it. I did a big anti-riot poster afterwards that was sold in the shops. I started getting disillusioned with America and I wanted to go back to Europe, so we came to England.'

There are many reasons a person leaves their homeland. For Gilliam, it was, in part, simply following his girlfriend back to her home, but there was also the allure of the artist in exile. In the late 1950s and early 1960s, several American directors Gilliam admired had turned their back on the Hollywood machine and decamped to England. Stanley Kubrick and Dick Lester were amongst them and made perfect company for an aspiring filmmaker. More important was the desire to put as much distance between himself and the Vietnam War as possible. Europe also offered romance and history, while America just seemed to offer riots and immoral 'police actions.' It would be thirty years before Gilliam returned to explore those troubled times in both his nation's and his own past, in his adaptation of Hunter S. Thompson's *Fear and Loathing in Las Vegas*.

Ironically, immediately before he left Los Angeles for London, Gilliam was offered his first shot at the movies, albeit in a non-directing capacity. A friend, who was working on the Tony Curtis vehicle *Don't Make Waves*, offered him a small part in the film, but it required Gilliam to cut his now long hair back into a crew cut. 'I'd had a crew cut most of my life, so I said no,' says Gilliam.

The anti-police riots poster — 23 June 1967

There was still the minor consideration of the draft to overcome, although Gilliam was already giving the U.S. Army a bureaucratic runaround worthy of *Brazil's* Ministry of Information. 'When I did my first trip to Europe, my ex-roommate was living on Rhodes so he became my mailing address. I got out of the National Guard when I said I was going to Europe, so I was put into a control group which was based in Germany but I was claiming to be living on this island in Greece. Eventually, I came back to America and this ridiculous communication was still going on. The army would write me from St. Louis, Missouri, to Germany, then it would be sent from Germany to Greece, then from Greece to New York, and eventually when I went back West, from New York to Los Angeles. I would respond to it, seal it in an envelope inside an envelope and send that to my friend in Greece, who'd then mail it from Rhodes to Germany, from where it was sent back to St. Louis. This went on for years.

'When I finally moved to England, the war was getting really hot and they were closing down all these control groups, and insisting everybody return to America. By then I had enough contacts. I was getting the BBC, [producer] Humphrey Barclay, the *Sunday Times Magazine* – basically, everybody I could get – to write letters saying I was essential to the continuation of their companies. And I got a lawyer here to say that if I went back to the States I would be indigent, there'd be no way of

(Right) A variation on American Gothic

supporting myself. I got an honourable discharge from the U.S. Army for behaving so dishonourably.'

Initially on his return to London in 1967, Gilliam turned once again to illustration work on magazines. He became art director on the short-lived *Londoner* magazine, but quickly tired of the work and decided to look up John Cleese in the hope of finding some way into television. Cleese had subsequently become something of a TV personality, as one-third of David Frost's comic on-screen entourage (the other two being the Ronnies, Barker and Corbett) on *The Frost Report*. He put Gilliam in touch with producer Humphrey Barclay, who had produced the original *Cambridge Circus* stage show and was now establishing himself in television comedy. Barclay was only mildly impressed with Gilliam's written sketches, but was intrigued by his artwork, being a cartoonist himself. 'I've always been able to carry around a portfolio of my work.' remarks Gilliam. 'That's the great thing about cartoons, you can carry them around, and Humphrey was an amateur cartoonist who loved the sketches.'

Barclay bought a couple of Gilliam's written pieces for the TV show he was then producing, a groundbreaking children's show that was achieving a cult following amongst adults, *Do Not Adjust Your Set*. The cast and writing staff included fellow Pythons-to-be Michael Palin, Terry Jones and Eric Idle. 'There was a certain amount of good old British middle-class envy there.' Michael Palin recalls of his first meeting with Yank-about-town Gilliam. 'Terry had this amazingly impressive coat, one of those great furry coats, and apparently lots of girlfriends and all that. We thought this glamorous figure had swanned in from America, and I think there was a certain amount of wariness bordering on envy there.'

Barclay also found a spot for Gilliam on camera, on Frank Muir's first series for the newly formed London Weekend Television franchise, *We Have Ways of Making You Laugh*. 'Humphrey got me drawing cartoons of the guests.' Gilliam recalls. 'It was that format of a group of people all sitting around being clever and witty and "Oh what have you done this week?" I was the quiet one sitting there. drawing cartoon caricatures of the guests. I turned Bill Oddie into a singing frog.'

A few weeks into the show's run, one of the writers, Dick Vosburgh, came in with a recording of several weeks worth of pun-heavy radio links by 'housewives' favourite' DJ Jimmy Young. The tape was clearly funny but no one knew what to do with it, how it could be presented on the show. Gilliam's suggestion was to finally earn him the longed-for way in to the world of filmmaking. 'I said let me make an animated film of it. I had £400 and two weeks to do it in, so the only thing I could do was do what I do – cut-outs. So I got pictures of Jimmy Young, cut his head out and drew other bits and pieces and started moving the stuff around, wiggling his mouth, and this stuff that Dick had collected was the soundtrack, and I just made funny animations of him doing things – his head coming off and so on.

'I knew everything and nothing,' Gilliam explains of his first attempts at animation. 'We had always done flip books so I knew that. Like somebody who picks up a guitar and can play it, I could just do it. In New York in the early 1960s I'd seen this underground film of cut-out animation and the thing I remember from it was Nixon's head, a newspaper and suddenly a foot in his mouth as he tried to talk. They were crude cut outs and I thought "That's what I'll do. I'll have to do it that way." I even think I had Jimmy Young put his foot in his mouth. So I did this thing and it went out on television and ten million people saw it. Nobody had ever seen anything on television like it and I became an animator. Just like that.'

Gilliam's work was indeed a unique sight on British television, with the crude cut-outs set against the rounded airbrushed backgrounds that would become his trademark. 'They were really fresh and different and really funny,' recalls Michael Palin. 'It was the 1960s of course, and a lot of people were doing all sorts of things with graphics. But Terry's were really funny. That's what struck me most forcibly first time around, and they never let you down. He was amazingly consistent.'

The style, Gilliam insists, came out of necessity, but even at this early stage it was more or less completely formed in terms of the work he would later do on Python. 'That's the way I am – if it works, why not do some more like that? Everyone liked it. I think it was the crudeness and the outrageousness that did it. I was always looking for free things, so I'd go to the library. There's a lot of dead painters and a lot of dead engravers, so we could use that stuff, start playing with it. I guess that's where my art education came from. I'd go down to the Tate, look through the collections, photocopy things and start moving it all around. The style developed out of that, rather than there being any planning. I never analysed the stuff, I just did it the easiest way. I could use images that I really loved. I could cut them out and move them about.'

It was this fondness for traditional art that, in part, defined the nature of Gilliam's early animated work; the sheer irreverence of a style that left old masters cut to pieces by the young upstart. 'It comes from drawing a moustache on the Mona Lisa,' he readily agrees. 'That's what it's all about, and to me it's always two things because I really love the stuff but I also find it funny. If you take it out of its pompous context there's a nice combination of reactions and emotions, so I worked like that. Because you're dealing with old paintings, you have kings and queens and beautiful Italian

(Above and opposite) 'Christmas Cards,' an early animation

masters and you start fucking around with them. And then there was the airbrush. Again, it was like picking up an instrument and playing it immediately. Nobody ever taught me any of that stuff; I just knew that I could do it.'

Gilliam did a couple more animated pieces for *We Have Ways of Making You Laugh* and Humphrey Barclay was so impressed with them that he enlisted his talents for the second series of *Do Not Adjust Your Set*. Having initially befriended Eric Idle – he, too, was impressed with Terry's sheepskin coat – Gilliam now found himself accepted by both Michael Palin and Terry Jones. Indeed, Jones was greatly taken with an animated piece called *Elephants* that Gilliam did for the series. Palin was equally intrigued by another piece, called *Christmas Cards*. 'It was absolutely brilliant,' the actor and occasional world traveller recalls, 'with missiles coming out of church steeples. Terry's stream-of-consciousness animation was one of the examples of a way of doing things differently.'

When *Do Not Adjust Your Set* ended, Gilliam provided another cartoon for one of Marty Feldman's shows, some illustrations for an early Ronnie Barker series, and the opening titles to the Vincent Price horror movie, *Cry of the Banshee*, of which Gilliam remarks, 'It's not that good, to be honest. Demons rising up and stuff.'

John Cleese, meanwhile, had been approached to do a series for the BBC. Along with his writing partner Graham Chapman, he was keen to work with Michael Palin. Palin brought his writing partner Terry Jones to the mix, along with Eric Idle. Still intrigued by *Elephants*, Jones suggested Gilliam. It was a case of Cambridge meets Oxford meets Occidental. The result of this combination was to be a show called *Owl Stretching Time*, and the genesis of the Pythons.

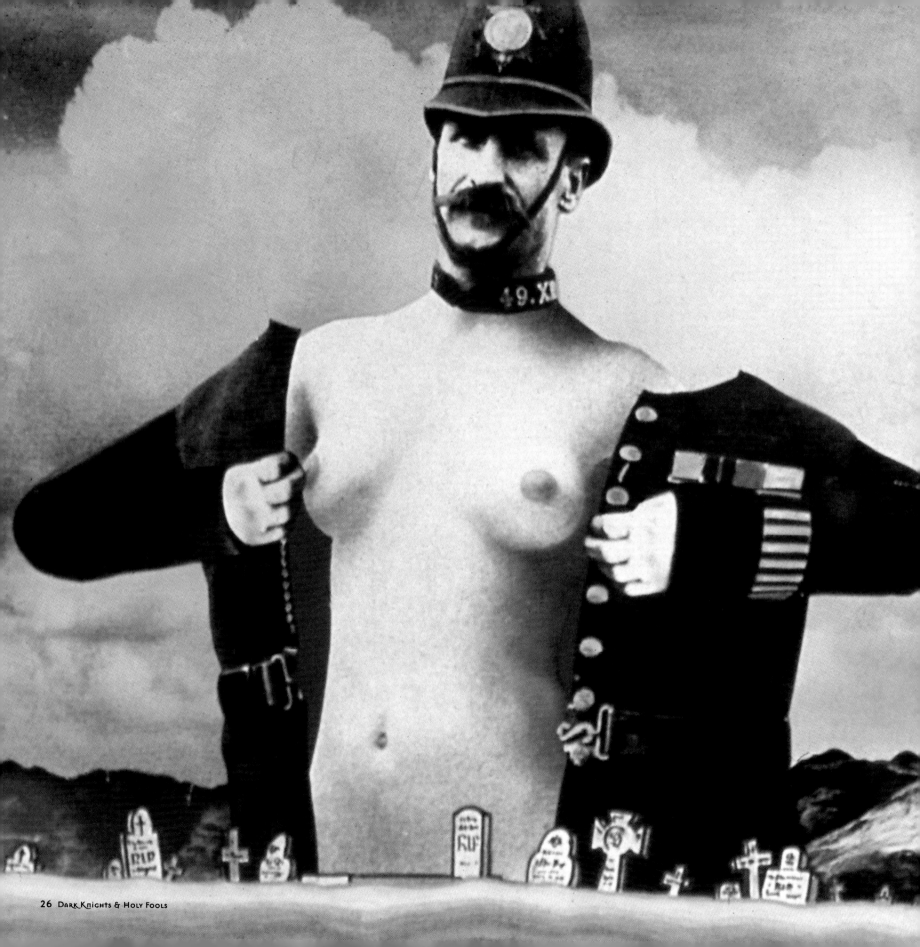

Monty Python's *Flying Circus*

ADVERSITY, NATURALLY ENOUGH, BREEDS HUMOUR. To coin an understatement, the Second World War was a time of great adversity. The comedians who entertained throughout the war came to dominate British comedy in the years that followed. But one old soldier, a touch more AWOL than most, changed all that. Spike Milligan, left shell-shocked by his experiences in the war, conceived and wrote a radio programme called *The Goon Show*. Performed by Milligan, Peter Sellers, Harry Secombe and, initially, Michael Bentine, its anarchic blend of multi-character comedy and surreal humour became, arguably, the most influential programme in the history of British broadcast comedy. As would be the case with *Monty Python's Flying Circus*, however, Milligan didn't influence his peers as much as the children who were listening to his show. Throughout the 1950s, these kids made their way through the post-war education system to university. When the likes of Peter Cook met up with Dagenham's own Dudley Moore, they found they had several things in common – they were teenagers in a society that now called them 'teenagers' and they loved the Goons. 'I used to go sick every Friday to listen to *The Goon Show* in the sanitarium. There was a sort of understanding between me and the matron,' Cook once recalled of his days at public school. 'I remember my parents and my aunts – it wasn't that they couldn't stand *The Goon Show*, but they always thought it was very loud – however much the show was turned down they still thought it was loud.' In his second year at Pembroke College, Cambridge, Cook auditioned for the university's legendary Footlights revue, which resulted in him devoting the majority of his time to writing and performing, rather than to his degree.

In 1960, Cook and fellow Cambridge alumnus Jonathan Miller teamed with Oxford graduates Alan Bennett and the piano-playing Dudley Moore to take a show to the Edinburgh Festival. Normally, revue-style shows played the 'Fringe' festival that had sprung up around the main event. But this was to be a late-night comedy revue, given the respectability of the official Edinburgh Festival. Jonathan Miller once recollected that, at the initial meeting between the foursome, they instantly disliked each other and decided it might be a profitable enterprise.' And thus, *Beyond the Fringe* was born.

Gauging the full impact of *Beyond the Fringe* is difficult to do now, but at the time the show represented a revolution, not just in British comedy but in British society in general. Here was a show that dared to lampoon the hitherto holy cows of the once-great Empire, be it the legal system, the war itself, or simply the prevalent attitudes in the country at the time.

When the show arrived in London in May of 1961, the effect was sharply felt and the satire boom was born.

Also attending Oxbridge during this period were five young men who, with the help of an American animator named Terry Gilliam, would change the face of British television comedy forever. John Cleese arrived at Downing College, Cambridge, in 1960. He joined the Footlights Club, where a year later he met new member Graham Chapman. In 1962, Eric Idle went up to Cambridge, becoming the president of the Footlights Club in 1964. Oxford did not have any club comparable to the Footlights, but it did have a tradition of college 'smoker' concerts and of revue-style productions. Terry Jones joined the university's Experimental Theatre Club, who traditionally presented an end-of-year sketch show. Here he wrote a sketch – a commentary on a custard pie fight – that would later become a staple of Monty Python's live shows. The sketch was written in conjunction with another student he did not know very well at the time, Michael Palin.

The satire boom moved on to television in the form of the groundbreaking *That Was the Week That Was* (*TW3*) and *Not So Much a Programme, More a Way of Life*, both fronted by Cambridge graduate David Frost, who debuted another show, *The Frost Report*, in 1966. *The Frost Report* tackled a major topic each week and took the form of an ongoing monologue delivered by Frost, interspersed with sketches performed by a trio of regular players – Ronnie Barker, Ronnie Corbett and John Cleese. Cleese's last Cambridge revue, *A Clump of Plinths*, had transferred to London in 1963 with the rather more mundane title of *Cambridge Circus*. The show then toured New Zealand before transferring to the Plymouth Theater on Broadway, where it unexpectedly closed, and ending up at the Square East, a smaller theatre.

In the audience one night was the assistant editor of *Help!* magazine. Impressed by Cleese, Terry asked him to appear in one of his *fumetti* strips. After a brief stint working for *Newsweek* magazine, Cleese found himself back in London and appearing on *Frost*. He also teamed with Graham Chapman as part of the show's writing team, alongside the double act of Michael Palin and Terry Jones and the solo output of Eric Idle. Marty Feldman headed the writing team.

David Frost was one of television's earliest entrepreneurs. He created a stable of talent, and then diversified. Both the two Ronnies ended up with solo series courtesy of Frost's Paradine Productions, while Cleese and Chapman were hired to write the movie *The Rise and Rise of Michael Rimmer*, eventually made in 1970 as a somewhat weak vehicle for Peter Cook. Frost also wanted a show for Cleese and fellow writer Tim Brooke-Taylor. Chapman and Feldman were added to the mix and the result was *At Last the 1948 Show*, one of the two true precursors of Monty Python. The other was *Do Not Adjust Your Set*. When John Cleese introduced Terry Gilliam to the *Do Not Adjust Your Set* producer Humphrey Barclay in 1968, the circle was complete.

The Frost Report moved to the newly founded London Weekend Television in 1968 and became *Frost on Sunday*, but John Cleese did not go with it. Nervous of performing on live television, Cleese

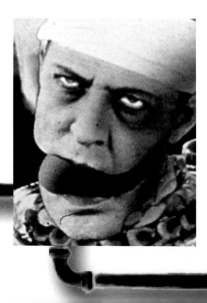

The Monty Python team, 1970.
l-r: Terry Jones, Graham Chapman,
John Cleese, Eric Idle, Terry Gilliam,
Michael Palin

had opted to devote himself to writing. His place was occasionally filled on air by Michael Palin who,
along with writing partner Jones, was writing and starring in the 'mockumentary' series *The Complete
and Utter History of Britain*.

Cleese was still very much in demand and the BBC let it be known that if he wanted to do a
show, they would be more than interested. Graham Chapman was already on board, and Cleese
was interested in working with Michael Palin. Palin brought Jones and Idle along, the three of them
having decided they wanted to keep working together after the demise of *Do Not Adjust Your Set*.
Together these five gathered to discuss the possibility of a new show. They wanted to do something
different, but were not sure what form it should take. Then Terry Jones remembered Gilliam's
animated pieces, especially *Elephants*. If they could just get that stream of consciousness effect and
apply it to sketch comedy, they might be onto something. Cleese and company were intrigued.

'When we were talking about the shape of a new show that eventually became Python,' says Palin.
'We were looking around for ways of putting a comedy half-hour together and Terry's stream-of-
consciousness animation was one way of doing things differently. I think his animations became the
thing which enabled us to do that format, because he could bridge us from sketch to sketch.'

'The six of us just sat down and started throwing ideas around,' says Gilliam. 'Mike and Terry would
write together, and John and Graham would write together, whereas Eric and I were on our own. We
would then come together with all these ideas and things we'd written and, little by little, the thing
would form. It was a totally unique time. The six of us all agreed to work together openly, without any
leader or anyone trying to push things along.'

The BBC, confident in the abilities of all concerned, bar Gilliam – who had so far worked
exclusively for the 'other side' – commissioned thirteen episodes of the potential show, not bothering
with producing a pilot. The question was what to call the series. *Owl Stretching Time* was one
suggestion, as was *A Horse, a Spoon and a Bucket*. Cleese toyed with the idea of calling it

Bunn, Wackett, Buzzard, Stubble and Boot, a lift from an earlier sketch of his. The words Flying Circus cropped up, and to them Michael Palin added the name Gwen Dibley (a name he had seen in a copy of *Women's Institute* magazine). *Gwen Dibley's Flying Circus* never materialised however. Instead the words Python and Monty were added.

The group came together, stockpiled material, and then tried to find the format to present it in. It was here that Terry Gilliam came to the fore. In part inspired by his earlier love of Ernie Kovacs and his surreal comedy shows, Gilliam saw his animation as the key to finding the show's new style. Soon all were in agreement, eager to break what they saw as the tyranny of the punch line. 'We'd never actually worked out how we could get away from the sketch show format,' says Palin, 'And although some of it was done with odd cuts and things, a lot was actually sewn together by Terry's animation.'

The first episode of *Monty Python's Flying Circus* was broadcast on 5 October 1969, late on a Sunday night. Viewers were greeted by Michael Palin's castaway 'It's...' man, then Gilliam's animated titles, accompanied by John Phillip Sousa's march *The Liberty Bell* – an interesting choice made by an American in self-imposed exile in Britain. What followed included tree-bound sheep labouring under the impression they were actually birds, a man with three buttocks, a mice-banging musical interlude and a disgruntled miner who ran off 'down t' pit' to avoid the theatrical leanings of his paterfamilias. The final voice-over announced that the existence of God had been proven by two falls. Safe to say,

Flying

British television had never seen anything like it before, which was not necessarily considered a good thing with the BBC, who took the show off after four weeks in favour of the *Horse of the Year Show* (which ironically featured Sousa's *Liberty Bell*). But by then it was too late: Python had already found its audience.

Modern youth culture had begun to find its numerous voices in the 1960s. Music had catered to this emergent group from the beginnings of rock and roll, with the Beatles and countless others evolving along with their audience, sometimes leading them, sometimes finding themselves in the same place at the same time. Movies had finally caught up in 1967 with *The Graduate*, the first mainstream movie to address both the alienation of youth and concede the whole notion of a 'generation gap', and also the first film to score itself directly to rock music, courtesy of Simon and Garfunkel. Later, in 1969, *Easy Rider* consolidated the generation on screen. When television dared to tackle the subject of youth culture, it was generally in the form of jaw-droppingly out-of-touch BBC documentaries with middle-aged men in suits making the most of their expense accounts while standing on the corner of Haight Ashbury saying things like 'They call themselves "hippies" and the message they send is one of love...'

Television had so far failed to address, involve or even come close to satisfying this new audience, but *Monty Python's Flying Circus* began to redress that. More than anything, it was subversive. The fact that something so unstructured in its humour could be representing the venerable BBC was, in itself, a turn-on for viewers. There was something about Python that defied perfectionism. Over its four-year run of forty five episodes, Python lurched from brilliance to banality, but in a curious way this was always a case of 'never mind the quality, feel the attitude.' What counted about Python was the fact that it was in there, doing it. You came along for the ride, or you didn't get the joke. 'At the time there was always that feeling that somehow there was a great audience out there,' says Gilliam.

'And that if you got it right, you could appeal to everybody, but we gave up on that idea. Ultimately we were appealing to just six people – us. If it made us laugh, it went in; it really was simple. Our attitude was very arrogant and that's what I like about the shows. We were just pleasing ourselves.'

While it is true no one expected the Spanish Inquisition, it is also true that Terry Gilliam's animations were something of a surprise in themselves. They had been seen briefly on other shows, but on *Monty Python* Gilliam's cut-outs became the dominant visual force. Given the fact that he was more of a surrogate performer on Python than his team-mates, Terry Gilliam's contribution to Python is often undervalued. In reality, if there can be said to be a designer of the whole style of Python, then it would be Gilliam. He provided the initial means to break from the norm in terms of the

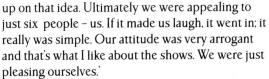

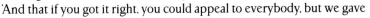

From Gilliam's book Animations Of Mortality

sketch show, and throughout the writing process provided the only truly unbiased point of view towards the material (a sort of comedic Switzerland, situated somewhere between Oxford and Cambridge). His often ferocious visual ideas hugely influenced the material being written by the others. Could a sketch involving a dead parrot being banged on a counter to display its 'ex' status have got by on a show that didn't have cartoons featuring an ambulatory cancerous black spot? Probably not.

At its best, *Monty Python's Flying Circus* was the outpouring of six brilliant minds, freed from the constraints of everything around them in terms of their upbringing, what had gone before and what the so-called rules were supposed to be. At its worst, the show was exactly the same thing. George Harrison feels that Python was the spirit of the Beatles transferred to six comics, and he may well have a point. The cult of Python quickly spread, and by the end of the second series, the group took to the road, playing the show live on stage in England and Canada where it had rapidly become a hit. Record albums followed. Beginning with the appropriately titled *Another Monty Python Record*, the group eventually produced eight albums (including film soundtracks) and, in 1980, took Harrison's Beatles notion to its natural conclusion by playing live at the Hollywood Bowl.

The Python team recorded two shows for Germany, but had a difficult time cracking America where some savagely re-edited broadcasts led them to sue the ABC network. Being the only American citizen amongst them, Gilliam led the claim, which became a forerunner of his later battles with such entities as Universal Pictures.

By the third series of Python, John Cleese decided to call it a day. Much as he had done back on the Frost shows, Cleese had tired of performing. 'I wasn't even that keen to do the second half of the second series,' he once said. 'I felt we were repeating ourselves.' By now, however, the Pythons were eager to expand into film. Their first effort, a re-filmed sketch compilation entitled *And Now for Something Completely Different*, was designed to break them into the American market, but singularly failed. They succeeded, however, with 1974's *Monty Python and the Holy Grail. Monty Python's The Life of Brian* appeared amid much religious controversy in 1978, followed by the Cannes award-winning *Monty Python's The Meaning of Life* in 1983. On the eve of the troupe's 25th anniversary in 1994, Graham Chapman died.

BOB McCABE: Eric Idle was the first member of what would become the Monty Python team to take you under his wing.

TERRY GILLIAM: Yeah, Eric liked my big Turkish coat. Eric's always been the one in Python that gravitates to outside, exotic talent quicker. He was the one that knew George Harrison, Paul Simon and Mick Jagger. I turned up with this great sheepskin coat and long hair and an American accent and I was obviously someone of interest. Mike [Palin] and Terry [Jones] were always much more territorial, they pull back, and so Mike and Terry are my best friends because I'm territorial too.

BM: How involved were you in the group writing sessions?

TG: The way it would work was that everyone would start off by going off in their separate groups. And then we'd come back and read the stuff out. The problem with me was that my ideas were difficult to describe and the others would just look at me aghast. After a while it became clear that I should just leave it and wait until it was a finished thing. A lot of the stuff came from them saying 'Well, the sketch goes to here, Gilliam takes over and gets us to here.' To me it was the greatest freedom imaginable, to have a start and an end and be able to go any-where in between. Once we had the scripts, which would be fairly rough and full of 'Gilliam takes over here,' I would just have to go and start cracking away while they'd be off filming, and I would maybe turn up for one or two days filming, just because I was feeling a bit out of it. I wanted to be part of the group, so I'd put on some piece of armour and do something stupid and then get back to work. Then on the day of the show I'd turn up with a can of film, and in it went. In many ways I was the luckiest of the group because I didn't have to have my stuff edited by the others. They just trusted me. Working on it, I would have at least one all-nighter each week. I was working seven-day weeks like a madman. It was all just stuff, paper and images, and at some point they'd start arranging themselves, which was very simple. At three or four in the morning you get pretty funny.

BM: Where were you working on the animation?

TG: I was living down by Putney Bridge, on the Fulham side, and I had an apartment there and a small workroom. When I was ready, I'd take all the stuff down to the BBC, use their rostrum cameras and shoot it. There would be a day of filming and I would prepare all the work before. I was working in a field of about thirty inches, which is big, because they're just pieces of paper. You'd be constantly trying to get rid of the shadows and packing things underneath the backgrounds. It's a really slow process, and the way I was doing the cut-outs was just inherently crude. The movements were always jerky. I'd also be doing the artwork, rushing down to Atlas Photography in Regent Street, where I was getting all these pictures from art books photographed, and they'd blow them up to the size I wanted. Then I'd cut them out and colour them in with felt-tip markers, then I'd airbrush a body, and so on. I'd have drawers full of grounds, full of skies, machines — all these bits and pieces. In many ways it was like a big proper film studio with the scene dock and the props house and the costume departments. It was pretty efficient. I look back and I can't believe I was producing 2-2½ minutes a week. I don't know how I did it because most of the time I was just working on my own. It was crazed.

BM: Your ability with airbrushing helped define the look of the animation. It gave it a more rounded texture.

TG: Airbrushing wasn't popular then. It didn't take off until the late 1970s. I just loved the fact that I could get very round things on film. I'm always trying to make things round — it's the flatness of film I don't like and somehow by airbrushing I was able to do that. I'm always in a rush, always trying to do more than I've got the time or the money for, so it's this constant battle of only going so far and then saying 'OK that's it, I've got to move on.' I don't know if I'm ever capable of taking things to the utterly refined level that some people do, because in the end I don't care that much. I care about the overall thing and that's what happened with the cartoons. There's an overall effect with engravings, airbrushing and photographs — all these different techniques and media squeezed together into one thing. And that kind of collage work is something I couldn't even do now because I need the pressure of having to turn it out each week to be as free as that. Now if I was given the time, I'd try to make everything just perfect, which doesn't mean better.

BM: How technical is timing a laugh with animation? Take, for example, one of my favourites, the old woman who fails to catch two buses and trips up the third. It's the pause that makes it work. Do you time that literally by counting frames, or it is more instinctive?

TG: It's all about pauses. What I would do is do the first bus going by and then do a very long hold. I would leave these big pauses in because I didn't know what the timing was when I was shooting it. I knew roughly what it should be, but I never trust my sense of timing on the spot. I think I'm better when I can actually retreat from the moment and get into an editing room and get it right. I had to give myself lots and lots of space that I could later edit out if necessary.

BM: Did you do your own editing?

TG: Ray Millichope was the editor of the show and I would just go down and say 'Here it is, cut there, take that out there, and there'. Editing has always been crucial in the films, whether I'm doing it myself or someone else is doing it. I have to be there. I don't under-stand how films get made where you hand it over to the editor and they just go and do it. I think there's a lot of directors who don't have a sense of timing. For all your ability to communicate or not, there are still times when you have to get your hands on that thing and just do it.

BM: As well as their distinct visual style, sound was very important to the animations.

TG: I listen to them now and the sound is so crude because I was doing it at home. The sources of the sound were the BBC library of sound effects and the rest was generally me just sitting in a room with a blanket over my head and a microphone, making noises. The sound is, I'd say, around 50% of what you're doing, and people don't recognise that. It's like the Python theme, [Sousa's] *The Liberty Bell*; that was my choice. We were going through material and that came up and I said 'that's it', because I could see animating to it. Now you only think of it as the Python theme, nobody thinks of it as *The Liberty Bell*.

BM: There was a strong level of violence to the cartoons you did for Python. Where did that come from and how aware were you of the violence in them?

TG: My excuse for that was because of the cut-outs. They're such simplistic things, that's all I could do. I couldn't do beautiful, articulated, sweeping, lovely things. All I could do was crude, and crude things ended up being violent, somehow. Right from the beginning, the foot coming down and Wham! — you create something beautiful and then you crush it. A lot of them are about that. I was in that phase where I was smashing things and it was funny. That kind of violence always seemed very funny to me. It was also at a time when the world was very anti-violence because the war was on.

I remember the premiere of *Holy Grail* in New York and the scene when the Black Knight came on and his arms and legs get chopped off. The whole audience gasped.

They thought it wasn't funny because it was about violence, and violence couldn't be funny. There was something in me at that time because I was so anti the war — that made me turn it on its head and use it in a very different way. I don't know why, but I was constantly exploding things and crushing things and blowing things up and ripping things apart and sucking things dry — it made me laugh. At least I didn't hurt anybody.

BM: Having successfully avoided the draft, and decamped to England, just how aware were you of the Vietnam War and did it influence you on a day-to-day level?

TG: One of the reasons I left America was the political violence that was going on, police riots, all that. I had reached the point where I either had to be a full-time activist, which I didn't really want to be, or get out. The only decent thing was to get out. People forget how violent and awful that war was. It was interesting on *Fear and Loathing*, looking at old war footage from that time — 1971, because nobody sees those images now, but they were our daily diet then. Now, the war images we get are Sarajevo or Rwanda, but it's very different when your own people are over there, smashing other people who shouldn't be smashed.

BM: One of the key images in the Python opening titles is of a network of metal pipes. It's an image that seems to have been with you ever since. In all your movies there's a fascination with the mechanics of how things work, often to the point where the workings are exposed on the outside.

TG: It's the innards of everything, whether it's people or machines. The inner workings of things have always intrigued me. Toilets have always intrigued me. I'm curious about how things work, how the guts of a system function, and the sound of plumbing is always comic. That's the thing I like about Python — it goes from being incredibly intelligent to incredibly infantile. What I think we're good at avoiding is the middle ground. We swing from really, really hip smart stuff to really childish stuff. I think that's what was good about us. We were always pushing it one way or the other. So we'd either fall flat on our face or fly high.

BM: What was the reaction from both the BBC and the audience?

TG: Initially from the first audience, it was just shock. They didn't know what it was. Then there was just the sound of hundreds of jaws dropping, it seemed to me. It was this middle-aged, middle-class audience that was in there and they seemed completely flummoxed by it. The BBC didn't know what to make of it either. They kept changing the time and the day of it so that you had to hunt for it, almost. I'm still amazed at the speed with which interest in the show took off. It felt to me that it was real grass roots stuff, and there was a groundswell that didn't come from any marketing or sales strategy. People found it and got excited. There was always that sense with Python, once it got stabilised on Sunday nights, that on Monday when you got to work, everybody would be talking about it. That's what you get out of television that you don't get out of films — millions of people experiencing the same thing at the same time. I think something fantastic happens when that occurs. Having said that, I think five years later Python wouldn't have happened.

BM: Were you affected by the Oxford/Cambridge divide?

TG: Oh yeah, because I'd always end up with Mike and Terry — Occidental, Oxford, practically the same. It's heightism as well because Mike, Terry and I are all about the same height; John, Graham and Eric are all over the six foot mark. Emotionally, I go with the Oxford side as well because they're much more conceptual, much more humane as people; they're not as tight-assed as the Cambridge lot. The Cambridge lot are so competitive and defensive and their defensiveness takes the form of aggressiveness, not like these nice little guys from Oxford and Occidental. It was so fortuitous that the six of us got together because we balanced each other really well. You couldn't have put together a better balanced group. Or a better unbalanced group, as the case may be.

BM: But how important do you think you being an American was to the dynamic of Python?
TG: I don't know. I really don't know. It probably did help because my simple crude, violent nature was a balance to their cleverness. I don't know if it was me being an American or my particular brand of energy in the way I see things. I think what might have helped was that I was such an Anglophile that I would fight them. Like in *And Now for Something Completely Different*, John would say 'We've got to say "canned peaches" for America.' I would say 'No, you've got to say "tinned peaches." It's an English word and Americans will have to learn what tinned means. And they will learn and get excited by the idea of learning. I would always throw back at them the time when the Beatles were doing 'Penny Lane' or any of those songs. I didn't know specifically what those songs were talking about, but I understood them and I wanted to learn, and I said, 'That's what we should be doing. Not coming down to them, make them come up to us.'

So on one level I was very useful to them because John was always trying to understand the audience so he could control them. I just fought with him all the time on that. I just thought he was wrong. And he thought I was wrong. But that's what was good about Python, we had these very strong opinions. It wasn't about compromise. Everybody got very passionate in the meetings and there was all this screaming and shouting, but we all respected each other enough to scream and shout at each other. That's the way it should be.

BM: Was there any level of censorship in Python between yourselves?
TG: Not really, no. There was something I think John was behind once. [Series director] Ian Macnaughton got the blame for it, but I think John was behind it. We were doing a silly religious thing and there was a bit where some vicar was phoning somebody, and we followed the wires and they went up to the next telegraph pole and there was the crucifixion of Christ with the telephone lines going through Jesus' arm, and that was the one thing that bothered John. I have no idea why. That was probably one of the few moments where he snuck behind our backs and got in there.

On the third series, the BBC tried to censor stuff. It proved to be an indication of how fucking sick their minds were, not ours. There was a scene where John thrusts his severed leg through a door to have it signed as a delivery for something, and in this meeting with [BBC1 Controller] Paul Fox he was talking about this scene where a man pushes his giant penis through the door. *What?* It was a severed leg, but they saw a giant penis. So we went through this whole fucking thing and I think he was embarrassed in the end, because we were a terrible gang. I would hate to be the controller and have the six of us walk into his office, like we did. Actually, when the show went out as a repeat on BBC 2, they censored two things. They censored the 'Proust Summarising Contest,' where one contestant's hobbies were golf, strangling small mammals and masturbation, and they beeped 'masturbation.' Then there was one of my cartoons where a prince has a spot on his face which he didn't tend to, and years later it turned into a cancer and he died — and they changed cancer to gangrene, because 'cancer' had become a word you couldn't make a joke about. What an extraordinary time, that in a repeat on BBC 2 you couldn't say 'cancer' in a cartoon.

BM: Was Python in any way influenced by drugs?
TG: No, that's what was interesting about it. The underground press at the time always thought we were druggies. I remember *Oz* magazine coming round doing interviews; they all just thought we were drug-heads. At best, I think there was a little pot smoking, that was about the extent of it. Drugs make me crazy, so I don't need them. That's what was funny about the time — everything was put down to drugs. That's how you were able to do things, with drugs. You couldn't do things because you were talented, because you were disciplined, because you were working your ass off, because you were experienced. You did it because drugs did it for you. The main drug of use was Graham's alcohol consumption, that was it. We were never druggie humour. It's undergraduate, juvenile, sophomoric humour.

BM: Finally, how do you think your work progressed during the whole period of Python?
TG: I don't know if it did progress because I never wanted to be an animator, and as the films and everything else progressed, I just didn't want to be the guy doing the animation. I was into live action films. That's what happened with *Jabberwocky*. Once I'd escaped from animation and got to where I'd wanted to be for a long time, I didn't want to go back. I don't know if they got better or worse within the shows. I think the first series is as good as anything, and when *And Now for Something Completely Different* came along, it was like 'Wow, films!' Then when the *Holy Grail* came along, that was it — Bingo!, here we go.

(right) Original artwork from the Monty Python opening titles

And Now For...

The classic Dead Parrot sketch, reworked in And Now For...

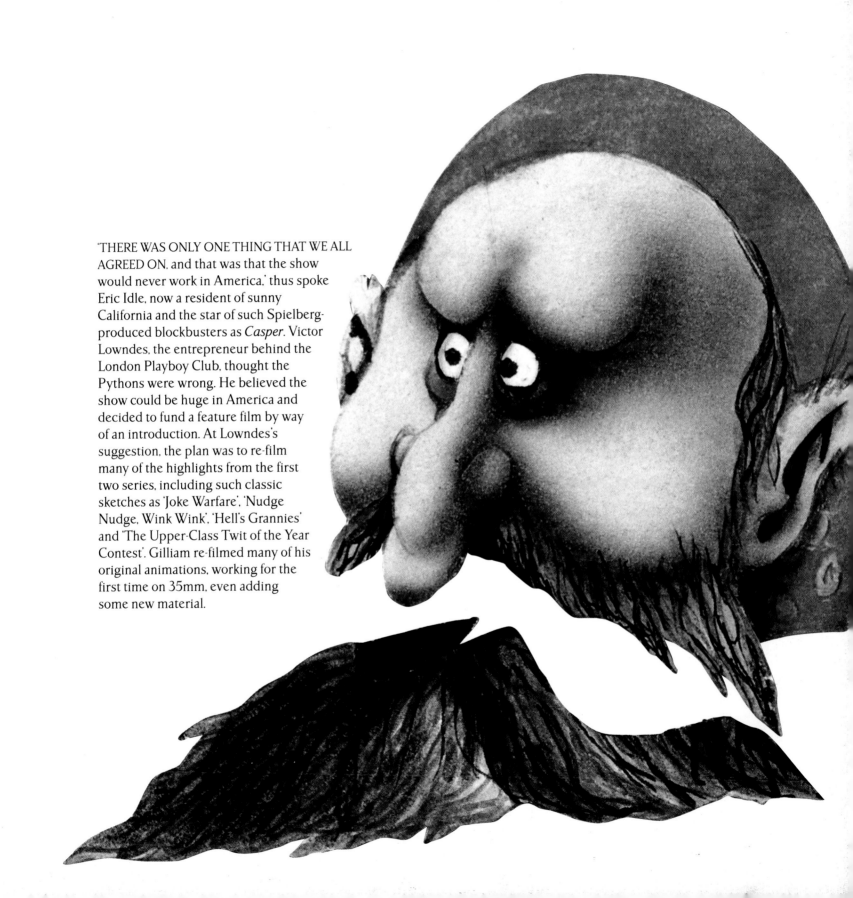

'THERE WAS ONLY ONE THING THAT WE ALL AGREED ON, and that was that the show would never work in America,' thus spoke Eric Idle, now a resident of sunny California and the star of such Spielberg-produced blockbusters as *Casper*. Victor Lowndes, the entrepreneur behind the London Playboy Club, thought the Pythons were wrong. He believed the show could be huge in America and decided to fund a feature film by way of an introduction. At Lowndes's suggestion, the plan was to re-film many of the highlights from the first two series, including such classic sketches as 'Joke Warfare', 'Nudge Nudge, Wink Wink', 'Hell's Grannies' and 'The Upper-Class Twit of the Year Contest'. Gilliam re-filmed many of his original animations, working for the first time on 35mm, even adding some new material.

Something

And Now for Something Completely Different began its five-week shoot in October of 1970 at a former dairy in north London. Its budget was a minuscule £80,000. The material and performances were more than up to scratch (the production notes describing the team as a 'half dozen immaculate anarchists'), but for both the cast and the audience, the movie remains something of a disappointment, lacking the energy of the TV shows and let down somewhat by Ian Macnaughton's pedestrian direction. 'It was frustrating because Terry Jones and I were always in there wanting to be directing,' Gilliam explains. 'Ian was lovely but he wasn't directing in the way we wanted it directed, and we were always saying "Oh come on, Jesus, shoot it this way," and it didn't quite happen. So there was always a certain frustration building up.

'We always seemed to end up having fights somewhere. It's funny, I don't have fights anymore, but in the early days you're always trying to establish your patch so you keep getting in fights with everyone. To me, the whole point of making these things is to make your own mistakes. I don't want to make somebody else's mistakes because I can't learn from that. I can learn from my own mistakes. And that's a real simple principle I try to work on. I don't think anyone knows what the public wants. You just do things because they're good. And we always try to keep it as simple as that, but nobody seems to appreciate that it can be that simple. What was always interesting about Python was that it was always divided six ways, which was very simple.'

Completely

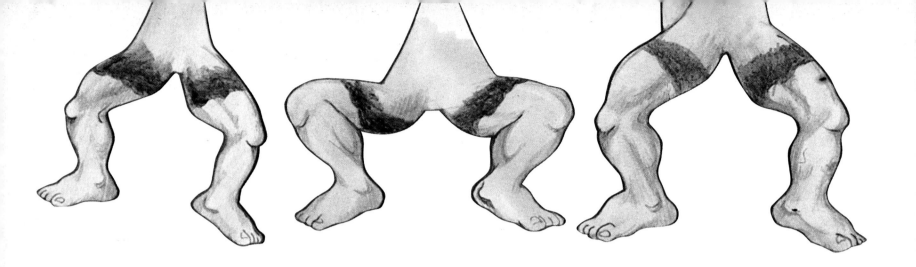

To add to the Pythons' general displeasure with their debut movie, the film flopped in America. Ironically, despite the familiarity of the material, the film became a big hit in Britain when it opened in December of 1971. Even more surprisingly, it became an even bigger hit in Japan in 1980. Here its latent release was accompanied by a twenty-page explanatory brochure that described the group as 'the Beatles of the world of parody.' This useful booklet also took the time to describe each scene in detail, for example: 'It is the middle of a Canadian forest; in natural surroundings a lumberjack cuts down trees, but in reality he is a homosexual.'

Despite the movie's box office success, some sketches left the Japanese audience a touch confused. The subtleties of Eric's 'Nudge Nudge, Wink Wink', originally written for Ronnie Barker to perform back in *Frost Report* days, lost just about everything in translation. Additionally, the 'Dead Parrot' sketch highlighted cultural differences: 'We Japanese wouldn't argue so much if a product was unsatisfactory,' a Tokyo girl explained to the *Sunday Times*.

Different

Monty Python and the Holy Grail

ALTHOUGH *And Now for Something Completely Different* flopped in America, Gilliam's animations had found another outlet in his homeland, via *The Marty Feldman Comedy Machine*. The man whose bug-eyed look had once left David Frost uncertain whether or not to put him on air, now found himself with a six-part sketch show on the U.S. network ABC. Given that *Monty Python* had failed to crack American network television, Gilliam's animations were a sight unseen on those shores, so the producers of Feldman's show commissioned twenty five minutes of new animation from him. The resultant pieces included his five-minute short *The Miracle of Flight*, the director's most sustained piece of animation, which later played numerous film festivals and was screened as part of the Hollywood Bowl Python shows in 1980. 'It was a total free hand to do what I wanted,' Gilliam recalls, 'and the nice thing was that it wasn't linking material. I could do set pieces, tell little stories. I did the opening credits, which are really good. I liked them a lot.'

As Python were facing their first censorship battles with the BBC, Gilliam found himself embroiled, typically, in another battle with ABC's standards and practices department. 'There was one thing I wanted to do on fat, and at one point I needed to have a Rubens nude in the thing, a classic fat, wonderfully fleshy creature, and they got a little bit nervous. The standards and practices lady was in her late twenties and she was overweight, about 180–190 pounds; not a happy, fulfilled woman. And she said "you can't do that." So I dug around and found another nude, back view. So in that goes and it comes back with the crack in her ass circled and a note saying "If you can cover that, maybe you can use it." So I said "Oh fuck this," and I got a Victorian nude postcard from Ronnie Barker, who collects them, cut her and her breasts out, stuck her on a background and asked, "Can I use this?" They said "No, because now you're drawing attention to the naughty bits." I couldn't show the naughty bits and I couldn't not show the naughty bits. So that's when I said "Fuck the lot of you, this is utter madness," and I went on a kind of strike. I did one piece of animation a minute long with nothing moving in it.'

The piece involved two characters looking at a dog that was 'playing dead' so convincingly that nothing in the frame actually moved. Ultimately, a hammer descended from on high and squashed everything. 'That was me in my violent mode. I just explode when I'm up against that mindless stupidity, and out of that anger sometimes come very funny things,' explains Gilliam.

Gilliam completed his commission for the Feldman show, which was his first real taste of dealing with the corporate media world outside the Python cocoon. 'Nobody was telling us "no" in Python. After doing it for several years and having the kind of success we had, for people to come along and say "no," one just goes crazy. It's very funny because it happened for years after. I want things to be out there. Once they're out there, people can decide for themselves whether they're good, bad or indifferent, but you've got to get them out first. To make television, films, books, whatever, you've got to run a gauntlet of editors and standards and practices people and studio heads to get it out – those are the people who infuriate me.'

More informed than chastened by his first Hollywood experience (although the show was shot at Elstree studios in the U.K.), Gilliam found himself back amongst the Pythons. Disappointed by everything but the box office figures for *And Now for Something*, the Python team decided to sit down and write a 'proper' film. 'What was interesting about the start of the movie [*Monty Python and the Holy Grail*] was how traditional we wanted to be,' says Gilliam. 'All of us wanted to make real movies, not Python movies, not the crap that we did.'

Since beginning the third series in 1972, the group had wrestled with the idea of such a movie. Somehow, all their collective pooling of material and debate over what this 'real' movie should be about had led to one of Gilliam's personal obsessions – knights. 'Once we decided it was going to be about King Arthur and the Grail, it seemed the perfect vehicle,' recalls Gilliam. 'You gather the knights together and we see all the characters, and you've got a structure that most people can understand – a quest. Terry [Jones] and I were great medievalists, so we couldn't wait to get in there.'

'Originally the first script of *Holy Grail* had the film as another Python mish-mash again,' Jones has said, 'half in modern day, half medieval. We had some time off, during which I thought to myself, "I'd much rather do it all medieval." I was in my Chaucer period at that time and I was surprised when everybody went along with it.'

A Cleese/Chapman sketch set in the Grail Hall in modern-day Harrods provided the spark, but all the Pythons found themselves enthused by the thought of taking on the Middle Ages. As with all their material, they were keen to examine the society of the times as much as they

Original sketch ideas for
Holy Grail **production**

were to simply churn out the gags. What were once termed 'sketches' soon began to emerge as scenes showing a world where oppressed peasants questioned the validity of monarchy, armed guards dispelled potential invaders with talk of the migratory patterns of swallows (and coconuts) and the presence of a king could be determined by the lack of shit on him. The reality of budget constraints meant that horses were not on the cards for this particular production. But who needs horses when you've got coconuts? 'The limitations put on us by the budget proved to be wonderful,' says Gilliam. 'We had to get clever and inventive, and thank God, because the coconuts saved our asses. We could never have got through that movie with real horses. And banging two coconut shells together for the sound of hooves is much funnier.'

As the writing progressed, it became clear that the team wanted full control, so the two Terrys stepped forward as potential directors. 'From the beginning I was very involved with the shape of the shows,' Jones explained to Python biographer Kim Johnson. 'I felt a very strong commitment to the finished product, actually seeing the thing through to the final edit. I don't think there was any desire to direct in the first place. It was just a result of seeing things get screwed up that we knew should be done better.' Terry Gilliam, however, had always harboured a desire to direct, and if co-directing his colleagues was the way to get there, what the hell? It was better than working your way up from teaboy.

With the script rapidly taking shape, West End impresario Michael White came on board to raise the movie's £229,575 (eventual) budget. Taxation for the average rock star income at this time in Great Britain was hovering around 85 per cent, so any rock star with an accountant worth his salt was looking to invest in tax write-offs. As a result, *Holy*

Grail was largely financed by Led Zeppelin, Pink Floyd and Elton John, forging a link between the Pythons and rock and roll that continued with George Harrison's involvement in *Monty Python's Life of Brian*.

Filming began on 29 April 1974 for five weeks on location in Scotland and Northumbria, with the two Terrys calling the shots behind the camera. Almost from the start, things started to go wrong. 'Two weeks before we started, the National Trust banned us from all their castles,' Gilliam recollects. 'The whole schedule had been based around the fact that we thought we had these castles, and they banned us because they said we wouldn't respect the dignity of the fabric of the building. So we had to completely re-jig everything, and it was chaos trying to find new locations with a week to go. We found this castle for the end scenes, one of the few private castles that worked for us. It was up at the top of Scotland and although that scene had been pencilled in at the end of the shoot, we had to shoot it at the end of the first week.

'So this madness started occurring. We didn't have the costumes because they were still in London, and so on. On the first day of shooting, Terry and I were all excited. We were at the Seven Sisters in Glencoe and all the vehicles were parked on the road, and we had to hump all the equipment down, across the river and up a mountain and finally to the Bridge of Death, which Hamish McGuinness had built up there for us. So we're ready to go, and then on the very first shot, the camera breaks. On my very first directorial shot. So what do we do? We do all the wrong things. We somehow manage to get another camera going and we shoot close-ups, which we could shoot in anybody's back garden. We're standing in the most magnificent scenery and we're doing close-ups. It was just madness, and we only got a few shots of the bridge.'

Despite the egalitarian nature of Python, the two Terrys were, to all intents and purposes, now team leaders, and this began to cause a lot of friction. 'The group actually started splitting internally,' Gilliam admitted. 'We'd always argued, but suddenly there were almost two groups. There was this group of four that were just acting, and the other two who were running around doing ten million jobs.'

Most vocal amongst the 'group of four' was Graham Chapman, who, despite being saddled with the relatively straight role of King Arthur, was drinking more heavily than ever before. 'I remember at the end of the first few days, Graham got drunk,' says Gilliam. 'Terry and I were trying to keep this thing together and Graham was howling at us about what useless fucking wankers we were and what assholes we were. Once again, Graham wasn't exactly right.'

'The problems were worst for the two Terrys, I think,' offers Michael Palin, looking back on the Pythons' first real big screen outing. 'The problem was thinking we could do it with two of them, which of course was fatal because we would play one off against the other. I remember one particular day at the end of the film, we were filming out on the water and Terry Jones was in full armour and the outboard on the boat he was in went down, so he was left drifting rather helplessly. So Terry G. grabbed the nearest boat, pushed off, and shot off after him. Unfortunately, his engine failed, so there was one point where both directors were drifting out on the water and this entire army of extras were cheering from the shore.'

Monty Python and the Holy Grail had its world premiere in February of 1975 in Los Angeles. Although each member of the team had accepted the relatively paltry sum of £2,000 up front,

their share of the profits from the movie would see them all very nicely, as the film rapidly became a huge success. Critical reaction, both in Britain and America, was also highly favourable. As a genuine first foray on to the big screen, the film was most certainly assured in its technical aspects, well acted and still true to its roots, not in terms of television, but in terms of the ethos of the group. If, at times, the Pythons seemed almost wilful in their inability to edit material, then that too was true of *Holy Grail*, but again, in such fields of comic brilliance, there is bound to be an occasional cow-pat.

From the opening shot (filmed on London's Hampstead Heath), the movie separates itself from the majority of British cinema of the early 1970s with its visual splendour. But amongst the grey skies and dark, satanic hills, amid the early morning fog, lies the heart of the movie its humour and its subversion. Into such a visually redolent background, complete with a suitably ornate orchestral score, the Pythons send a noble king... and a guy named Patsy banging two coconut shells together to make up for the lack of a horse. This one scene typifies the nature of the movie and, indeed, a good deal of Python humour. It is not so much parody as the constant undercutting of expectation; knowing the route, but taking the surreal off-ramp.

When Gilliam entered college in the U.S. he rejoiced at the fact that one could, 'start the jokes at a certain level.' He was in good company with these Python fellows, whose observation and corruption of language often fuelled their humour. Thus, a peasant defying his king is given added resonance by his offering up of a Marxist theory on the nature of class in 'England, 932 AD'. This particular scene highlights the unique balance between the Pythons as filmmakers and as writers. As filmmakers, the Pythons were at pains to create a real world. The attention to detail here, the dirt, the squalor, is practically unheard of in a comedy movie. Just consider how many corpses Eric Idle picks up in the 'Bring out your dead' scene before the gags even start. As writers, the Pythons used the language of the characters for their own ends, as exemplified in the line 'I didn't know we had a King. I thought we were an autonomous collective.' Indeed, these early scenes in *Holy Grail* are so successful at creating a world that they manage to cover over the fact that, for all its potential unity, the movie is, at times, little more than a series of sketches on a common theme.

Having realised that their visions were similar but disparate, Jones and Gilliam divided the directing chores up, with Jones largely dealing with the actors and Gilliam responsible for the camera. 'It's very hard to co-direct,' recalls Michael Palin. 'I think Terry J. has a feeling that there is a kind of Python unity that can be tapped anyway, whereas Gilliam is more of a loner and knows that a certain amount of dictatorship is probably required. That's the way he's worked. He's always been his own boss, so the two approaches didn't really work out. He also had a very strong idea in his mind of how he wanted films to look. Things could be moved about from place to place just to get the light coming through at the right time, and that wasn't the way to deal with the Pythons. John Cleese wasn't interested in the beautiful light catching his helmet as he kneeled in the trenches, and you couldn't really tell him otherwise. I think the great success of the combination is that we did get a really beautiful film in the end, but I think it was a very wasting process for the two Terrys.'

BOB McCABE: What do you recall of putting the *Holy Grail* together?

TERRY GILLIAM: I don't remember much about writing. Ideas were being thrown around and I think it was the sketch they wrote in Harrods that started it. But once we were on, it was OK. Everybody did their research and started writing funny sketches. Then we started stitching them together, so it looked like there was a story there. Then the thing I remember most was 'God, Terry and I are going to direct this thing.' My memories are about going on locations and roaming around England. We went to every castle in England, and we were working and getting costumes and stuff. That's the part that really excites me on films, the pre-production, because everything's possible. And then, of course, it all falls to rat shit.

BM: Does it always fall apart?

TG: Not as bad as it did on that one. I've gotten better. I know it's always going to, so I'm prepared now. But for me, there was a real tension there because I was trying to make this epic. And I had spent so long in my little room with pieces of paper that I hadn't adapted to talking to human beings and getting them to do things that I wanted them to do. I remember when we did the scene where they are at the battlements and the cow is thrown over, it was a matte shot and I had to keep their heads lower than the battlements. And the only way we could do it was to dig a hole in the ground and have them all on their knees, and John was going apeshit because he was uncomfortable. And I finally said 'Fuck it. It's your sketch, you wrote it. I'm just trying to make it work. This is a tricky shot here.' Finally I said 'Fuck you' and I went off in a snit and laid down in the grass. Terry and I, who had always sort of been one voice, suddenly realised we weren't. It ended up with Terry talking to the guys, and me talking to the crew and the cameramen and that side of it. It worked fine once we got that sorted out.

BM: Why was Graham so disgruntled?

TG: It was because he was a drunken sot, that's why. He couldn't say his lines as Arthur. He'd get through a sentence and then he'd blank out. This great dignified character is actually blotto and he's struggling to get through his lines. Graham was a mountaineer, he was a member of the Dangerous Sports Club, he was all of these things, but we came to do the Bridge of Death and he couldn't go across it. He just completely froze. So Gerry Harrison, the assistant director, had to put on his costume and double as Graham going across. What's so funny is that you're up in these very perilous conditions, somewhere on a mountain, and all the truth suddenly comes out — Terry and I don't know how to direct and Graham can't go across a bridge.

BM: Did having the two Terrys in charge throw the group off balance in any way?

TG: Ultimately it didn't, but it took some time to settle down. Both Terry and I had strong ideas about what we wanted to do, and after a while, some of the group didn't want to know. It suddenly seemed as if we were pushing everyone around, which we had to, in a sense. I always think the actors will have to go against us at some point, and we've got to go against them at some point because we're trying to do one thing and they're trying to do something else. But it didn't split the group in any way; it just shifted things. Most of the time it went really well.

BM: It seems an obvious thing to say, but it must have been unusual for you moving into 3D images after years of 2D animation.

TG: It was a change, but I needed one because what frustrated me about animation was that it was flat. That's why I was airbrushing it.

BM: How was it working with the other departments after years as a one-man show?

TG: That's where I was at my best because I really get on well with others. Because I can draw I can deal with the costumes and I can deal with the sets, and it was a chance for me to design all these things. Or supervise them at least. So we'd find the locations and [production designer] Roy Smith would start. [Costume designer] Hazel Pethig was brilliant too, because we didn't have any money. We started making tabards out of old cotton sheets and simply painted things on there. In a sense that's why the balance worked, with Terry talking to 'them', the others, and me dealing with all the other departments.

   The whole thing with films is working with really good people, because you get a lot more than I could bring to it if I was working on my own. It's a way of continuing to learn, working with people who can do things that I can't do. And they learn from me and vice versa.

BM: Although the movie does capture the reality of the period, it starts to deliberately mess with that reality — 'Scene 24' being introduced, the modern-day stuff, etc. There's a feeling of the film almost breaking down at those points, as if you didn't know how to sustain it.

TG: We wrote it that way. We were really playing with the medium. If I'd seen *Grail* and not made it, I would have thought it was wonderful because it was playing with the form. Which is what we were doing on television. We were never taken seriously by serious film magazines, and I think we were far more adventurous and avant-garde than anything else that was going on then. You look at Alexander Walker's *History of British Cinema* and we're a footnote at best, but you go to places like Belgium or the continent and we were huge. Python *was* British filmmaking in the '70s, if you travel around the world. But not in Britain.

He was a drunken sot... He couldn't say his lines as Arthur. He'd get through a sentence and then he'd blank out. This great dignified character is actually blotto and he's struggling to get through his lines. Graham was a mountaineer, he was a member of the Dangerous Sports Club, he was all of these things, but we came to do the Bridge of Death and he couldn't go across it.

BM: The movie uses some animation, but not much.
TG: Because it was like trying to do two jobs. I actually enjoyed doing the animation on that one, because for the first time I had more help. I had two assistants.

BM: Did you or Terry Jones take the dominant hand in post-production?
TG: It got very interesting. There were constant fights going on. I had one with Terry. The problem I had at the time was because Terry would look at a piece of film and would always seem to be reading too much into a shot. There were some sneaky things going on, too. I was coming back at night and changing the shots, putting back the one that I wanted. It happened a few times because I thought it was wrong. Terry was reading emotional information that wasn't on the celluloid. Terry gets very emotional about those things. He seems to think they have a life of their own. I don't think they do. It's a piece of film. It has X amount of information on it and that's all there is to it, and that's what you've got to look at.

BM: How was the movie received by your backers?
TG: When we showed our first cut of the film, people hated it and there were walk outs. This was a screening for Pink Floyd and Elton John and Led Zeppelin, and I think Graham or Eric walked out. The balance of the sound was wrong and there was such expectation and tension within the group, they thought Terry and I had completely fucked it up. We went back and re-jigged things but we didn't really change that much. We just balanced things better. I think at the time we were really obsessed with sound, and we'd built up too much atmosphere at times and it was getting in the way of the dialogue. We were so keen on creating this world that we fucked up.

Jabberwocky

BEWARE THE

(Above) A sketch of the
Jabberwocky. (Left) The director
in planning mood

TERRY GILLIAM'S SECOND EFFORT AS DIRECTOR, on
Jabberwocky, was in many ways an extension of his debut. Indeed,
for a brief moment it appeared that finally a filmmaker had
emerged to corner the previously undemographed 'medieval
comedy' market. 'That's how *really* stupid I was,' the director
laughs. 'We made another medieval movie that's a comedy to all
intents and purposes, with three of the Pythons, myself included —
now that's just stupid or arrogant, I'm not sure which.'

Post *Holy Grail*, animation was clearly on the back burner for Gilliam.
He finally had a taste of directing movies. Admittedly, working with
his friend and colleague Terry Jones had not been as satisfactory an
experience as it could have been, but the final film stood as testimony
to the fact that maybe, just maybe, he knew what he was doing.

Producer Sandy Lieberson thought so, and sought out Gilliam to
direct *All This and World War II*, an odd mix of war footage and
Beatles' songs (sung by recording artists of the day) that could really
only ever have been suggested as a project in that culturally uncertain
time of the mid-1970s. Although tempted, Gilliam passed on the
project, hoping instead that the BBC would put up the money for a
half-hour experimental piece, inspired by certain lines that were busy
whirling round the filmmaker's head:

'Twas brillig, and the slithy toves
Did gyre and gimble in the wabe;
All mimsy were the borogoves,
And the mome raths outgrabe.

Beware the Jabberwock, my son!
The jaws that bite, the claws that catch!
Beware the Jubjub bird, and shun
The frumious Bandersnatch!

For the vast majority, Lewis Carroll's 1872 poem is a prime example of nonsense, a rhyming collage of manipulated language that a Python could easily delight in. For Terry Gilliam, it was a movie. 'It was actually the poem and the fact that there were all these ideas I'd had for *Holy Grail* that we didn't use,' Gilliam recalls of the film's origins. 'Nothing is ever straightforward when I approach it. The poem is basically nonsense. I love the sound of it. It's whimsical, it's musical, it's surreal, and it conjures up things with me, not just images, but it feels right. I also felt in *Grail* we were limited by the fact that we had to be funny and it was sketches all the time. I wanted to see if we could do a real narrative.'

Having had his dream *Beatles-meet-the-Hun* project rejected (it was made instead by Susan Winslow in 1976), Lieberson wisely asked Gilliam what it was he wanted to work on next, to which the debutant director simply replied, 'I want to make a film called *Jabberwocky*.' Gilliam's ideas for the movie still added up to little more than Carroll's verse and some unused Python material, so he enlisted the services of Charles Alverson, his predecessor at *Help!* magazine and a man once described by Michael Palin as 'co-writer, hippie and American "novelist".'

Alverson was living in Wales at the time, and Gilliam decamped to his place to work on the script. As with all of Gilliam's subsequent co-writing projects, the director laid claim to the ideas, the character and the situations, while his co-author tended to flesh these concepts out and add the majority of the dialogue. 'Sometimes I get the right line, but writing dialogue is not easy for me. It just doesn't come as easily as it ought,' Gilliam admits. Consequently, Gilliam and Alverson would be holed up for days at a time; planning, discussing, notating. Alverson would then retreat, turn the notes into script form, bring them back and begin the whole process again.

To some observers, Gilliam may have appeared to be deliberately setting himself up for a fall, taking on what was, at that time, only the second medieval movie comedy the decade had produced. But for him, the milieu was something he had craved since he was a child, a passion that had fuelled his initial trips, back in the 1960s, to the place he now considered home. 'It's an inability to grow up, isn't it?' Gilliam laughs. 'Knights, castles, princesses, dragons, things that have to be slain, quests to go on — this is basic Joseph Campbell country. Nothing changes, I've always liked that. I like the look of the times. I like medieval paintings. I like the way people's imaginations worked; I think they were much more vibrant. You weren't dealing with ego and id, you were dealing with something that looked like *that*. The place was peopled with strange forces and demons, and that kind of literalness. Anyway, if you're making films, those kind of visuals are just great. One of the reasons I came to Europe and stayed here was I saw real castles. The route that goes through me is childhood fairy tales, to Disneyland, to Europe and real castles, to making my own.'

Gilliam was, of course, in a quandary from the start with *Jabberwocky*. His reputation was linked with the Pythons: the financing of the film – a proposed budget of £505,000, which went over to the tune of a further £45,000 – was raised, in part, on the tacit agreement of the others making a tokenistic appearance in the film. Yet, in his heart, Gilliam didn't want to make a Python movie. As he explained to *Films & Filming* magazine back in 1977, 'I was never sure in

Behold, King Bruno the Questionable — probably the best film part Max Wall ever played

my own mind, even when we were shooting, if it was going to be a medieval film that was heavy on atmosphere, or an outrightly realistic film, or a Truffaut-type film that was basically straight but had moments of comedy, or an out and out comedy.'

Jabberwocky began filming on 26 July 1976. Over the following nine weeks, the production shot on location in Wales, at Pembroke and Chepstow castles and at Shepperton Studios, with Gilliam utilising the redressed street sets from the 1968 musical *Oliver* – the very set he had walked the day he'd scaled the wall at Shepperton years before, fantasizing about making the studio his own. Now, for those nine weeks, the studio was his own.

Cleese, Chapman and Idle had all declined to be involved and had requested contractual assurances that the Python name not be used in connection with the film. Fellow Python Palin did, of course, appear in the lead role of Dennis, the coppersmith's son, whose dreams of marriage to the girl next door are scuppered by the chance to become a monster-felling hero. The only other Python to appear was *Grail* co-director Terry Jones, and he was promptly (perhaps tellingly) dispatched in the first scene. 'I couldn't get rid of him quick enough,' laughs Gilliam, looking back. 'Truthfully, that wasn't the intention, but if anyone reads that into it, they're probably closer to the truth than not. Python made us and Python was everything, and everything we've done subsequently has been based on what Python did. But then you keep trying to get away from it so you bump 'em off little by little.'

One of the film's major achievements was to preserve a classic period of British comedy on celluloid. For anyone who grew up in Britain in the late 1960s and early 1970s, nearly every face in this movie is greeted with enthusiasm and fond memory. Max Wall was a variety stalwart, Harry H. Corbett was the titular offspring in *Steptoe and Son*, the incomparable John Le Mesurier was the main reason to watch *Dad's Army*, and Rodney Bewes was the one who wasn't James Bolan in the peerless *Whatever Happened to the Likely Lads?* An American director-in-exile managed to take some of his adopted homeland's finest televisual talent and transfer it to

the big screen. More importantly, having got the
actors there, the director allowed them to stretch,
as Gilliam recalled: 'I was a great fan of Max
Wall's. I thought he was breathtaking, it's the best
part he ever had and he chews up the scenery,
and the relationship between him and Le
Mesurier is wonderful because in rehearsal they
suddenly decided they were just a couple of old
queens. So all these things, like Le Mesurier saying "Oh my darling," just slipped out. It was such
a funny thing, I thought "Yeah, go with this one".'

According to Michael Palin, Gilliam's skill at
handling actors was definitely improving as he
went along. 'I think he was learning really, and I
think Terry would probably admit that's the thing
that has taken him longest to do. He has a very
high regard for actors, and what he had to do is
sort of, somehow, demystify them, but also find a
way of working with them that will produce the
best on both sides. Somewhere in the middle
there, Terry found the right way. So he could
ask actors to do something, but he could make
them understand clearly why he was asking
them to do it.'

As a former animator making the big leap to
directing 'real' people, Gilliam was eager to storyboard nearly every scene in his movie. It was a
technique he found useful, although as his career
as a filmmaker has developed, it is something he
has come to rely on less and less. 'One of the
things that happens with me is that when we're
writing it, I start drawing,' he says, 'the storyboard
to me is like writing. I start drawing it and I'm
telling the story in a different way because the
picture is telling me the story. In the act of
drawing it, I'm changing my ideas of what I'm
doing. And it's really magical when I get going.

'One of the problems that occurred was
because I don't draw figures with their proper
proportions and I get caught in this problem of

trying to force real proportioned actors into my frame. I always said that's why I started using dwarves in *Time Bandits*, because they're the proportions I draw people in... I was still insecure enough and relying on them [storyboards] enough during *Jabberwocky* that I was quite rigid on the studio floor, trying to get them doing it the way I had drawn it.'

Then, of course, there was the monster. When the young Terry Gilliam was watching *Ivanhoe* and other films of that genre, he was also devouring the stop-motion delights of Ray Harryhausen. One of the major attractions of *Jabberwocky* was the chance for the nascent filmmaker to create his own monster. The budget dictated that it was unlikely they would get beyond the typical guy-in-a-monster-suit routine, but Gilliam wanted to do more. The creature was to be played by Dan Muir, a 6' 8" university lecturer, so Gilliam and monster designer Val Charlton hunkered down, raided the local butchers for entrails, and came up with a grand plan. 'It was always the knees that gave it away,' Gilliam explains. 'So for my monster I turned the guy round in the suit, so that he was actually standing with his legs bent out behind. That was my great moment. Nobody's done it since. His arms worked the wings, so all we had to do was support the head, which we did off a cherry-picker with a cable. For the kind of money and time we had, it's a pretty good beast.'

Despite a later, erroneous, reputation as a filmmaker with no regard for budget, Gilliam, more often than not, looks for the most inventive but also most cost-effective way of doing things. The turning of the book pages in *Holy Grail* had been shot in the home of editor Julian Doyle, with Gilliam's wife Maggie starring as 'the hand', using a monster glove bought, mere minutes before, from a local joke shop. For the final scene shot in *Jabberwocky* – that of Dennis hiding under his shield from the creature – the entire cast and crew involved were Gilliam, his wife Maggie, Doyle and Palin. Maggie sorted the costumes and make-up, Palin performed on a refuse pile on the Shepperton backlot, Doyle blew smoke in from the side and Gilliam stood on a rusty old chair with a hand-held camera. 'Basically, we had to fake everything when we made *Jabberwocky*,' Gilliam relates. 'When John Boorman made *Excalibur*, I was told he showed *Jabberwocky* to the crew fourteen times. He got our armour and everything. For better or worse, we captured something very successfully and I like that.'

When the film was released in April of 1977, the critics agreed that Gilliam had indeed captured something; they just were not quite sure what it was. Ever the iconoclast, the director found himself caught between the proverbial cinematic rock and a hard place. Here was a movie made by a Python, but it wasn't a Python movie; it wasn't as laugh-out-loud funny as people expected. To reiterate the point, Gilliam chose to favourably compare his work with the densely-packed

canvasses of Bruegel and Bosch. Furthermore, he chose to point this out to American critics reviewing his film, which did not go down too well. 'Jabberwocky is not a grand enough failure to sustain such comparisons,' wrote Richard Schickel in *Time* magazine, before going on to conclude, 'It really is marked-down Pythonism, which proves that in enterprises of this sort, several heads are better than one.'

Nonetheless, many reviewers were in favour of Gilliam's second stab at directing, with the *New York Times*' Vincent Canby going as far as to call it 'a wickedly literate spoof of everything from *Jaws* through *Ivanhoe* to *The Faerie Queen.*' Sadly, Derek Malcolm's prediction in his *Guardian* review that 'it is one British film this year that will make a healthy profit on both sides of the Atlantic' proved incorrect, with the film underperforming at the box office, particularly in the U.S., no doubt due to the ultimate confusion of the Python connection.

An argument could be made that by revisiting the *Holy Grail*'s period, Gilliam was treading familiar ground, but if truth be told, he was simply trying to get it right as he saw it. 'It felt very much like Terry's vision of what he wanted the world to look like,' offers Michael Palin. 'It was not dissimilar to the *Holy Grail* in its de-glamorising history, but it felt very different from Python.' More than anything though, *Jabberwocky* was a transitional film – the shadow of Python loomed large, but the talents of its filmmaker were clearly emerging.

'One of the things I really wanted to capture was the atmosphere of the time better than we did in *Holy Grail*, and I achieved it,' says Gilliam today. 'I was trying to make a real Grimms' fairy tale, which are very bloody. I think that's what I was trying to achieve more than anything. I finally persuaded the distributors to show it as a Saturday morning film for kids and they loved it. I keep thinking kids are the most intelligent audience because of that openness to things. In a way, I guess, that's what I'm trying to do in all the movies, is to make adults kids again. To make them able to experience things the way that kids can.'

BOB McCABE: The film stems from Lewis Carroll's poem, but presumably it was *Holy Grail* that dictated the period of the picture.

TERRY GILLIAM: When it comes to filmmaking, the medieval period can bear comparisons with a Western. The archetypes are really clear. You know where you are. There's a hierarchy; a king, the serfs, and you can play with those. I liked the idea that it was two fairy tales on a collision course with each other. In the one fairy tale you've got the little guy who slays the monster and gets the princess and half the kingdom, and that's what we're supposed to all want. The other one is what he really wanted, which is the fat girl next door, not this other stuff. So he doesn't get what he wants and that's what intrigued me about it. The other thing that intrigued me about it was this man with very limited dreams

— he wants to marry the fat girl next door, he wants to run his shop and count his barrels and be a stocktaker. His dreams are so small and yet he's caught in a world where fairy tale endings are possible, but he doesn't get the happy ending he wants, he gets the fairy tale ending we're told we all want.

BM: Certainly in the films that follow *Jabberwocky*, it's easy to see you in your central characters, whether it be Sam in *Brazil*, the young boy in *Time Bandits*, in aspects of both the Robin Williams and the Jeff Bridges characters in *The Fisher King*, but I don't see any of you in Michael Palin's character, Dennis, in *Jabberwocky*.
TG: I think that's fair. I think it's the anti-me. It's growing up and being around the Dennis's. That's why I left; that's why I got away from people that had such small vision, limited vision. On the other hand, there's a sense of the character I like in that he heads out and gets caught up in adventures. Life takes over, but he really is my opposite, I think.

BM: You once described *Time Bandits* as the first official Terry Gilliam film. Where does that leave *Jabberwocky*?
TG: *Jabberwocky* was still caught in this semi-Python world of telling jokes in a jokey kind of way. I didn't feel quite as confident as I did in *Time Bandits*. I think I was still trying to escape from the sketch format and all that. I watched *Jabberwocky* for the distributors down at the labs and, for whatever reason, the soundtrack hadn't arrived and we watched it silent, and it was stunning. It looked beautiful, like a really serious medieval film, because the jokes were gone, and I thought it was almost a better film that way.

BM: There is a feeling in the film almost of two sides at battle — the one who feels obliged to be funny and the one who doesn't want to.
TG: That's right. That's what it was really about. It's taken a long time to get comfortable with the fact that I don't have to be funny all the time, that I can actually get in there and say things and still be watchable and entertaining. It would be interesting to re-do that film. I'd have to re-write it, but I could see it would be a really beautiful story.

A typical Gilliam poster treatment

BM: Given that it was your first experience of directing performance, how well did you respond to that?
TG: Watching Bergman films and such, I think, 'God, how do they get these great performances?' And I've still never worked it out. As a director, I spend all my time in pre-production talking about it to them, so I really get to know the actors and we all try to get into the character. It's a two way thing. But basically when you get into it, it's trying to

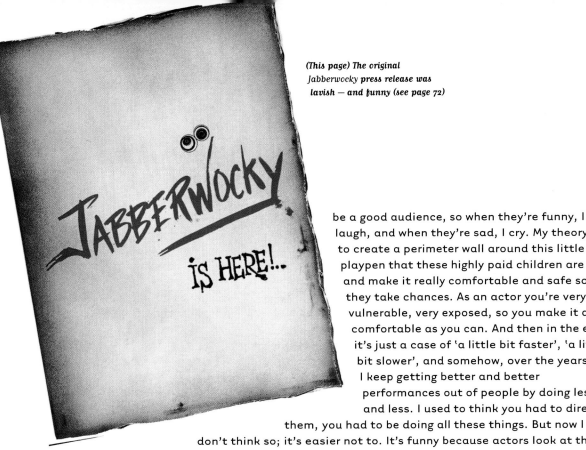

(This page) The original
Jabberwocky press release was
lavish — and funny (see page 72)

be a good audience, so when they're funny, I
laugh, and when they're sad, I cry. My theory is
to create a perimeter wall around this little
playpen that these highly paid children are in,
and make it really comfortable and safe so
they take chances. As an actor you're very
vulnerable, very exposed, so you make it as
comfortable as you can. And then in the end
it's just a case of 'a little bit faster', 'a little
bit slower', and somehow, over the years,
I keep getting better and better
performances out of people by doing less
and less. I used to think you had to direct
them, you had to be doing all these things. But now I
don't think so; it's easier not to. It's funny because actors look at the
films and they see other good performances and assume I'm a good director. I let
them assume that and try to keep my mouth shut.

BM: It's true, you are thought of first as a very visual director, but as
the career has progressed you've become more and more of an
actor's director.
TG: That's what's really happening. That was the break on *The Fisher
King* after *Munchausen*. I'd gone to the heights of visual madness
and then pulled back. I think I was getting really good performances
right from the beginning, but nobody ever noticed it because they
were too busy talking about the visuals or the comedy, or whatever.
Read reviews of *Brazil* and they just mention Jonathan Pryce in
passing. Jonathan holds the whole fucking film together but
nobody seems to notice that. They're talking about the sets and
angles, but that's bullshit. All that is there, but it's Jonathan
that's making the film work and they miss that.

BM: When looking at the two movies, there's a sense that *Holy
Grail* is stylised fantasy and *Jabberwocky* is realistic fantasy.
TG: I like that. I'll agree with that. I was always trying to keep the
characters' feet on the ground. So in the case of the castle,
they're building and repairing this old structure that's collapsing.
I remember at a press conference once, someone asking if it was
a metaphor for Thatcher's Britain, or if the *Jabberwocky* was
Communism, and there's something in that. *Jabberwocky* was

influenced by *Gormenghast*, Mervyn Peake's book. So you've got a castle that's in a continual state of crumbling and being repaired, and there's always workers in there. So you've got a king that has to walk around with dust falling in his food and the north tower always collapsing, all those things. There is a reality there somewhere, however stretched it is. That's why Dennis's father is a craftsman. He makes barrels and barrels are hard to make, so Dennis just wants to be a stocktaker. That's where I think the monetarist, mercenary, mercantile approach of Thatcher was creeping in on the thing. One was doing a job well and one was stocktaking.

BM: It is one of the few movies that actually shows you what it was like to live in a castle.
TG: I know. We had no money. So for the big sets we hired some rubber flagstones, but we could only hire a few, so we'd put them down on the floor and just light those areas. The walls we managed to get enough rubber and plaster stones to go up to about eight feet. The rest is black drapes. People thought Python had made millions, but Python never made the kind of money anybody thought it made because we were working at the BBC, and even the film didn't make much money. But people thought there were Python millions and that *Jabberwocky* should be a big budget film. There'd be a moment like where Bernard Bresslaw was getting out of jail and we didn't have a set. We had a door, some bars and one of our windows. And the crew were screaming, 'but this is not a set,' and I said 'I don't need a set, I need a window, blackness and some bars and you see his face and hand come through and that's all you need. It tells a story.' It's really hard to get some people to think like that. It's a test of how good the actors are, and we basically pull it off each time, but it's a non-stop battle.

BM: What is interesting about the scene in the armourer's workshop is that it does relate to the constant use of tubing and plumbing and that tracking shot at the opening of *Brazil*. But you're not looking at the machine; this time the humans are the machine itself.
TG: This comes out of the same idea as *Brazil*. The cogs are always human. I think people use machinery as a way of avoiding machinery, but still somebody either is the machine, or is in control of the machine or has bought the machine. It's always intrigued me how people are the system, and not the technologies.

BM: Once again there's violence in the humour. For example, Harry H. Corbett meets a particularly unpleasant death, squashed under a bed by the man he's just cuckolded.
TG: That intrigues me because it's a really fine line — how far can you go? I don't really know where that line is, so I'm experimenting with it

all the time. You do that in a cartoon and nobody would think twice. But can you do it
with real people, and how do you do it? I suppose it's the way you set the scene up in
advance and the way Bernard Bresslaw leaps through the air, because if they just
rolled onto the bed and crushed him it wouldn't work. So it's got to be a fast, cartoon
way of doing it.

BM: The first cut of *Jabberwocky* was reportedly lower on humour and you re-cut it to
up the gags.
TG: I was panicking. It's that awful moment when, having finished the editing and
thinking it's there, you start showing it and it's not going. So I kept pumping it up. It's
being caught in other people's expectations that drives me crazy — and they'd seen
Holy Grail and I was supposed to be funny.

Great Unmade No.1:
Gormenghast

TERRY GILLIAM FIRST READ MERVYN PEAKE'S *Gormenghast* trilogy – *Titus Groan*, *Gormenghast* and *Titus Alone* – in 1976. He focussed his attention on the middle book of the series, *Gormenghast*, originally published in 1951, and translating it to film instantly appealed to him. Gilliam clearly connected with Peake, the late author himself having been a famed and influential illustrator, most notably of Lewis Carroll's *Alice's Adventures in Wonderland*, a key text for the filmmaker. In subsequent years, Gilliam's desire to make a movie has rarely coincided with the rights being available or being in the right hands at the right time. However, the influence of Peake's *Titus Groan* trilogy can clearly be felt in the crumbling castle locations of *Jabberwocky*. 'I'd read *Gormenghast* before, so *Jabberwocky* was, in a sense, my attempt to do *Gormenghast*,' he admits, 'but it [the rights] kept coming and going. Different people had it at different times. At one point Peter Sellers had it; he was going to be Prunesquallor. Then there was a guy who had the rights to it but had never made a film before and I said I could get it made, because at that point I was a guy who could. I had a burgeoning career. But he wanted to hold on to it, so that went again.'

At one point Gilliam's London neighbour, the rock star Sting, had acquired the rights, with the intention of playing the role of the villainous Steerpike, and was all but banging Gilliam's front door down to persuade the filmmaker to come on board. 'At that time, to be honest, I didn't feel he was quite right for the part,' Gilliam says, though Sting eventually played the role in a radio production of the trilogy. 'Around the time of *Time Bandits*, it [*Gormenghast*] floated up again. It keeps coming at me and scripts keep turning up. I ultimately think there's such wonderful stuff in it, but people keep stealing it. If you look at [Ridley Scott's] *Legend*, there's a scene in a kitchen that's straight out of *Gormenghast*. It's almost better to use it as a quarry.'

A copy of the book jacket still takes pride of place on the notice board in Gilliam's home work-space, but he has long abandoned the notion of bringing Peake's masterwork to the screen. 'I think it's a hard thing to do because there's not much of a story there. It's the atmosphere and characters that are wonderful. Ultimately, I'd think I'd rather steal from things than actually make them. It's only been later in life that I've been foolish enough to actually make the thing. It's always been better to steal.'

Monty Python's
Life of Brian

THE IDEA OF ANOTHER PYTHON MOVIE was first suggested in Amsterdam on a promotional trip for *Holy Grail*. 'We were on a pub crawl one night, and I remember Eric sitting down and coming up with the title "Jesus Christ, Lust for Glory," and we fell off our chairs, it was just so funny,' remembers Gilliam.

Eric Idle repeated the gag during the American leg of the press tour and that the next Python piece would tackle religion seemed inevitable. Religion was a subject that quickly appealed to the group as a whole, all of them eager to draw on their own varied upbringings and backgrounds. 'That's the good thing about the group. For all of the internal competitiveness, a good idea does win, and people had great respect for a good idea,' says Gilliam. Early meetings showed they were all united on one thing – Jesus Christ was not the way to go. 'Very quickly we came around to the feeling that Jesus was OK, so we weren't going to take the piss out of him. He was genuinely OK,' Gilliam says. Ironically, for a film that produced screams of 'blasphemy!' on its release, the Pythons had decided right from the beginning that they didn't want to be blasphemous. They had toyed with the idea of someone who went round pretending to be the Holy Ghost, impregnating the Virgin Mary and palming her off with lines like 'Don't worry I'm a messenger from God', but this avenue was also rapidly abandoned.

Gilliam and Idle, torturers supreme

Thus, Brian was born. The first draft of the screenplay, provisionally titled *The Gospel According to St. Brian*, was ready by Christmas 1976. At that point Brian was the previously unsung 13th disciple of Christ, the one

The Pythons, 'writing' in Barbados, 1977

who handled the money and booked the dinner reservations, but nearly always managed to turn up late for all those big events like the Last Supper.

But even in this form, the Pythons weren't happy. Jesus was still a strong presence and none of them felt they wanted to direct their humour at him. Eventually, they decamped to Barbados for a two-week working holiday and here *Life of Brian* finally came together. Brian was now in no way aligned with the Lord. He was, as John Cleese once described him, 'just a bloke in Judea in 33 AD.'

As before, the writing of the movie began with the group breaking down into their component parts and writing various short scenes and sketches on the subject. But, perhaps due to their mutual enthusiasm for the topic, these individual pieces, for once, formed into a strong cohesive narrative. 'More and more it became about organised religion,' Gilliam recalls. 'It became about the followers, the people.'

With the script in place and the money (£2 million) coming from Lord Bernard Delfont's EMI, the *Life of Brian* cast and crew were all set to go in April of 1978. This was a Wednesday, a bad day. Apparently somebody at EMI finally got round to reading the script, and by Thursday the film's funding was gone. Filming was due to start on location in Tunisia two days later.

The hunt for new financing delayed the start of production until the following September. During that time salvation came in the unlikely form of a former Beatle. Eric Idle had met George

Harrison while promoting *Holy Grail* in L.A. They had become friends, with Harrison even joining the Pythons on stage for 'The Lumberjack Song' at their City Center concert in New York in 1976, right around the time the first draft of the *Brian* screenplay was being put together. Idle asked Harrison if he would be interested in investing in the film. His response was to form Handmade Films with business manager Denis O'Brien, which became one of the most prolific and successful British production companies of the following decade.

Two references are made in the finished film to these varied financiers. George Harrison appears as Mr Papadopoulis, 'the gentleman who's letting us have the mounts on Sunday,' while Eric Idle refers to Lord Delfont in his spoken outro to 'Bright Side of Life': 'I said to him Bernie, I said, they'll never make their money back.'

Gilliam arrived on location in Tunisia in the summer months of 1978 to oversee set construction in his new capacity as the film's designer. The others joined him in early September. After his frustration with *Holy Grail*, and coming off what was, for him, a far more successful experience on *Jabberwocky*, Gilliam had opted not to co-direct alongside Terry Jones. However, even this situation didn't quite work for Gilliam: 'You can design all you want, you can plan, you can storyboard it, and then the director either shoots it that way or not. We'd built all these sets, like Pilate's palace, and we spent a lot of money on it, and then it's not on film because Terry shot it just like a TV thing.'

Gilliam's design ideas were certainly elaborate. The old part of Pilate's palace featured three levels, the new part only two. 'It was something about two cultures clashing in the architecture,' explains Gilliam. Although these ideas were discussed and accepted by the group, when it came to filming the movie, such background details were often left off-camera. 'We were just shooting the scene, which is ultimately the right thing to do. But if that's all we're gonna do, we shouldn't spend the money building all this other stuff. I hate waste in a film. Some of the big shots that really look good are ones where I put the camera where it should be, because Terry was in the scene.'

Filming began on 16 September in the city of Monastir, and it was a remarkably relaxed shoot for all those concerned. The heat of the Tunisian desert was a sharp and

Unused poster art for Brian

welcome contrast to the memories of *Holy Grail*'s rain-swept highlands.

One large-scale scene in the movie involved 450 locally recruited Tunisian extras, all required to laugh at Pilate's speech. To warm up the crowd, the production enlisted the help of a local comedian. On asking Gilliam what such a being is like, he remarks, 'Bad. Like a Butlin's Redcoat.'

One of the most significant events to come out of *Life of Brian* was Gilliam's meeting with the actor and writer Charles McKeown. 'I was working as an actor,' McKeown recalls, 'and I met Michael Palin and Terry Jones in Sheffield where I did a couple of short plays of theirs [*Underhill's Finest Hour* and *Buchanan's Finest Hour*]. As a result of that, when they were going to Tunisia to do *Life of Brian*, they were looking for a group of actors to come along and play all the parts they didn't want to play. So I met Terry in Tunisia. He was this lunatic running around art directing in the midday sun, dressed as an Arab.'

'Charles did the most wonderful thing in that scene where Terry Jones is the hermit in the hole,' Gilliam fondly recalls. 'The crowd arrives, and Charles steps forward and says, "I was blind and now I can see" and falls in the hole, and that fall is breathtaking. He didn't do it once, he did it over and over again. I think that endeared Charles to me forever.' During breaks in filming, the two discussed the possibility of bringing *Gormenghast* to the screen, and at *Life of Brian*'s wrap party Gilliam told McKeown about the other story he was currently developing, *Brazil*, thus marking the start of future work together.

Gilliam's tasks as designer on *Brian* had left him little or no time for animation (although the title sequence remains some of his best Python work), and the rest of the group generally agreed that the narrative was strong enough to not need linking material. The one exception to this was the spaceship sequence, suggested by Chapman. This was filmed two months after the Tunisian shoot, with Gilliam constructing a small spaceship capsule complete with two aliens and, of course, the prerequisite amount of wiring, tubing and assorted inner workings. An ingenious, and decidedly low-tech affair, the scene works remarkably well, most notably in an impressive asteroid shower that was all filmed on the floor, without any post-production opticals. Months later, while promoting the film, Gilliam bumped into George Lucas (who had filmed much of *Star Wars* in Tunisia), who raved about the spaceship sequence. 'This was post-*Star Wars*,' says Gilliam. 'I said "Yeah, OK. We did it for a fiver".' Coincidentally, Lucas' next film, *The Empire Strikes Back*, featured an asteroid shower of its own, at considerably more cost.

Monty Python's Life of Brian was released in 1979 to a veritable tumult of protest. Banned in many parts of the American South, the film incensed Bible belters who had never actually got as far as watching it, but still found time to picket the film's U.S. distributors, Warner Brothers. As a result, the American box office suffered. Similar protest in Britain – where the Bishop of Southwark and commentator Malcolm Muggeridge memorably debated Cleese and Palin on late-night TV — had the exact opposite effect, with fans and new (dare I say it) converts flocking to see the movie.

And rightly so, for *Life of Brian* remains the Python's crowning achievement, featuring the group working at both their sharpest and, off-camera, most harmonious. The film wittily lampoons a variety of types (indeed, those protesters should look a little closer here), with the Python's familiar fascination with anachronistic language at its height. Similarly, the movie also offers the best performances the group as a whole have ever given, something that director Terry Jones wisely makes the most of, opting for long single takes for the majority of scenes and really allowing the performances to play out.

Perhaps more than anything else, *Life of Brian* was the perfect synthesis of all the Pythons' individual styles and unique ambitions. Although written as individual sketches, the film forms a complete and cohesive narrative. The visual realism that Jones and Gilliam particularly aspired to is present in the film's striking locations, atmospheric images and Geoffrey Burgon's suitably dramatic score. In short, *Life of Brian* looks so much like the religious epics it sets out to subvert that the jokes just seem funnier and funnier. And with Eric Idle's 'on the cross' singalong, 'Bright Side of Life', the film delivers one of the most outrageously memorable climaxes in modern cinema.

BOB McCABE: Why didn't you want to co-direct this time?

TERRY GILLIAM: Terry and I, when it actually came to working, didn't see things in the same way. Having shot *Jabberwocky* with real actors and really enjoyed it, I felt directing Python was the dogsbody job. It was a constant battle: 'What do you mean I've got to wear this costume,' 'Why do I have to wear this beard?'

'I'm not doing this scene if there's smoke in it.' You get all that crap. I don't think John or Graham thought in filmic terms really. I think they just wanted to get out there, say the lines, be funny and be as comfortable as possible while doing it. Now there is nothing wrong with that; it's just not what I wanted to be doing.

BM: Was most of the writing work done on the trip to Barbados?

TG: Everybody had gone their separate ways and had written stuff, so it was just a case of hammering things out and coming up with new ideas. It was weird because we were in this villa that Winston Churchill used to stay at, a really grand place for six silly comedians. People sort of dropped in. Mick Jagger and Jerry Hall dropped in for a night of charades, Alan Price was down there, Keith Moon I think floated through at one point because Keith was going to be in the film. But you can say that a particular sketch was written by so and so: John and Graham wrote the Latin one, 'Haggling' I think was Eric, 'The Leper' I'm pretty sure was Mike and Terry.

BM: Had you lost interest in animation by then, or did it just not fit the movie?

TG: I was drifting away more and more. I mean, after having done *Jabberwocky* I didn't want to do animation again, period. I had always wanted to do live action, so I had finally achieved it and I didn't want to go back. I actually like the title sequence. I think I did a really beautiful thing. I'm pleased with that. The spaceship scene was a chance to do a live action, special effects sequence.

BM: How was the sequence shot?

TG: The whole thing was done in a little studio about twenty feet by twenty five feet, maybe even smaller than that, in Neal's Yard in London. I was doing everything in-camera. We did the asteroid shower — which is just bits of foam rubber that we cut up and painted — all in one shot. I had a track with the camera and I'd

put the thing against black velvet and it would be on a little spindle that we turned from behind the black velvet. I would then track in on it and make a map of where the track went — that quadrant would be taken up with that asteroid. Eventually I got about thirteen asteroids that never crossed each other and they're all coming at you at different speeds. We didn't have special effects guys, so we went down to a joke shop and got all the exploding cigars we could, dumped out the powder, made a little bomb, then broke a light bulb and used the filament as the firing device, and that's our explosion for the spaceship hitting the asteroid. The thing that made it work, that kept it funny, were the sound effects on the spaceship. I used a motorcycle mixed in with other stuff, with its gears shifting. You never hear spaceships shifting gears, and you know it's silly.

BM: The first cut was apparently around $2\frac{1}{4}$ hours [the released movie runs at 93 minutes]. What was cut?

TG: There were several key sequences that went. The one that I think was probably a mistake was the King Otto sequence — they're a suicide squad who turn up at the end when Brian is on the cross and kill themselves. [The suicide squad still make a brief appearance in the final cut.] And it's a scene about a Jewish suicide squad that are trying to build a Jewish kingdom that will last a thousand years, and I'd managed to take a Star of David and turn it into a cross between the Star of David and a swastika. In retrospect I think we should have kept it in, but I think Eric got cold feet because he was living out in Hollywood at the time and he felt the Jewish producers of Hollywood would take great offence at it. I said, 'Listen, we've alienated the Christians, let's get the Jews now.'

There was another scene at the beginning, with the three shepherds round the fire, talking about how much they love sheep. And in the background you see the star coming across, and the wise men going by, lights over the horizon and angels descending from heaven, while they're looking the wrong way, talking about sheep. Then there was a scene where they raid Pilate's palace and are trying to kidnap Pilate's wife, but she turns out to be this giantess and they end up running away from her. It was a lot of knock-about stuff.

BM: Were you surprised by the extreme reaction the movie received?

TG: I kind of thought we would get it. I remember when I was doing *Help!* magazine we did something with the Mona Lisa on the cover and we got inundated with these protests of how

Original title artwork for Life Of Brian

Designer Gilliam scouting locations, Tunisia, summer 1978

dare we defile the Virgin Mary. So I thought we'd stir it up. I thought it was good because it stirred up the right people. The very ones who are in the movie. I don't think we stirred up anyone who was truly religious. We stirred up fanatics basically, whether it was the Bishop of Southwark or not.

BM: Were you keen to get away from the Pythons at this point?
TG: I think *Jabberwocky* really spoiled me. I was probably pulling away from the group. I was keen to do one of my own. I decided that if we were gonna have a pattern, then it would be Python, then mine, Python, then mine. I was also working on *Brazil*, but it was going nowhere...

Time Bandits

'I APPROACHED IT AS A FILM that no one would be embarrassed to see,' so said Terry Gilliam on the eve of the release of *Time Bandits*.

Prior to this 1981 tale of epoch-marauding little people, Gilliam's work as a whole was the sum of its parts: hugely inventive, visually imaginative and coarsely amusing. In *Time Bandits* those parts found a new consistency. For all its diverse influences – and the movie takes in a range that mixes and matches Lewis Carroll, sixteenth century cartography, *The Wizard of Oz* and, inevitably, Python – *Time Bandits* found its form by its maker wholly immersing himself in what had influenced him the most: fairy tales. A high school prom king still holding on to the stories his parents had read to him is as difficult to imagine then, in the 1950s, as it is now, but Gilliam never let go of those tales of darkened forests, chivalrous knights and damsels in distress. Moreover, *Time Bandits* is infused with the heart and soul of any kid who ever spent time at the 'Saturday morning pictures'. Informed by that feeling, *Time Bandits* allowed its maker to forget the technicalities of the medium and concentrate on the heart of it. On *Time Bandits* Terry Gilliam really became a storyteller.

This being a Gilliam story, of course, nothing could evolve that simply, and the truth is that *Time Bandits* began life as *Brazil*. Late in the *Jabberwocky* shoot, Gilliam was formulating a new idea for a movie that would present some kind of timeless future view, an Orwellian world where pen pushers pushed everyone's buttons. At first it was called *The Ministry*, but was rapidly re-christened *Brazil*, in reference to the 1930s song Gilliam heard swirling round his head whenever he thought about the film. Tellingly, one of the first statements Gilliam made about the movie (to *Film Comment* in 1981) claimed that it was 'All about paranoia, and all about America.'

Having spent over a decade away from his homeland, Gilliam seemed eager to address the world he had left behind. His next three movies – *Time Bandits, Brazil, The Adventures of Baron Munchausen* – would, in their

David Rappaport costume tests,
plus (right) Gilliam's dwarf
audition notes, 1979

staunch defence of imagination over harsh reality, offer his explanation and riposte to America. In the next trilogy – *The Fisher King*, *Twelve Monkeys* and *Fear and Loathing in Las Vegas* – he would slowly, and somewhat unexpectedly, make his way back home. He was to look initially at the contemporary ills of that society, then examine its future and potential downfall, before finally heading off in search of the American Dream – something Hunter S. Thompson had failed to find in Vegas, circa 1970, and something Terry Gilliam had seen fade away during the L.A. police riots of 1966.

It is no coincidence that the protagonists of *Time Bandits* move backwards through the ages; time travel, after all, was something Gilliam himself had chosen to do in terms of his own background and country. He left America in search of the castles of Europe, lives in London in a house built in the 1690s and vacations in a twelfth-century Italian farmhouse. He is, in his own way, a time bandit. 'I keep going back in time,' he agrees. 'When I went to Egypt a couple of years ago I thought "This is it. Now we're getting warm".'

Gilliam co-wrote an early draft of *Brazil* with Charles Alverson. 'But we split after only about a month. I just felt we weren't going in the same direction. It wasn't the same relationship. It was possibly because it was getting jokey again, and I was trying to pull away from that.' After that, Gilliam inadvertently hit on the time motif by focussing his hopes on the story of Theseus and the Minotaur, but once again, no one was biting.

The Pythons were all shareholders in Handmade Films, so here was access to the cash he needed to become the filmmaker he wanted to be. The only thing missing was the right idea. Over the course of one weekend in November of 1979, Gilliam came up with the idea for *Time Bandits*. Popular belief maintains that this took the form of a six or seven-page 'treatment', but the document that remains in Gilliam's archive today is a fifteen-page piece that bears the title 'The Film That Dares Not Speak Its Name – A treatment... not a cure', complete with a hand-drawn cover of a ship emerging from the water atop a giant's head. This 'treatment', fleshed out over just a weekend, is at times remarkably faithful to the final film. Already present are the marauding Time Bandits, who appear in the room of a young boy (not yet named Kevin). They take him on a series of adventures through time, wherein they meet the likes of Napoleon, Robin Hood and Agamemnon, and then to the Land of Legends and on to confront Evil in the Fortress of Ultimate Darkness (though, as yet, unnamed). However, the original does differ from the movie in a number of ways.

The Time Bandits do not appear on the night after the knight emerges from Kevin's wardrobe, but instead Kevin finds his room flooded with water and a pirate ship appears that sails off through his bedroom window. The first encounter with the Supreme Being is not when the little people appear the *next* night, but during a future time travel to London in the year 2267, when the Supreme Being tracks Kevin and company down and chases them through time.

The original concept has the heroes travel through a forest of hand-trees, a scene that was not included in the film version. The final battle takes place in ancient Greece with the dwarves using the time holes to assemble a cross-millennial arsenal of weapons (in the final scene as it now stands), led by the recently-returned Agamemnon. This leaves Kevin alone to face Evil, who has by now transformed himself into a 'huge, black, horrendous creature – evilly swaying back and forth as it towers above him.' The screenplay concludes with Kevin back in his bed, being yelled at by his dad. Annoyed, he throws the last remaining piece of evil charcoal at his father, reducing him to a puddle of water. 'Whatever am I going to tell the neighbours?' says his mother, 'I just had his suit cleaned. It'll never look right on a puddle of water...'

The future sequence in London seems to have served as a temporary dumping ground for many of Gilliam's design concepts for the already existent *Brazil*. The London they arrive in is described in the treatment as 'a maze of metal pipes, conduits, tubings and towers. A grey, harsh place.' The workers in the 'central planner's office' dress in uniform dark coats and hats, much like Sam Lowry, while 'signs inform us that this is our future bliss they are planning.' A theatre driven round on a 'fork-lift truck-type vehicle' reminds one of the house-on-a-truck Jill delivers in *Brazil*.

Enthused by his weekend's work on the script, Gilliam took the treatment to Dennis O'Brien at Handmade. Determined not to let this one suffer the same fate as *Brazil* and *Theseus*, and aware of his own need to get another movie made sooner rather than later, Gilliam not only showed the concept to its potential producer, but took the time to act the whole thing out. O'Brien was suitably convinced, as was Handmade's George Harrison, and almost immediately Gilliam had a 'go' project. From Handmade he hopped a cab to Michael Palin's house to convince him to take on the scripting chores.

'I thought I'd got rid of him for a bit and that I'd have some time to myself and my family without Gilliam showing up with a wonderful film idea,' Palin recalls of Gilliam's pitch. 'Terry has such great visual ideas that it wasn't a film for a writer to really go to town on... I mean I didn't want the words to get in the way of the pictures,' Palin continues, 'It was the history thing I enjoyed. All the Pythons were always suckers for history.'

For Gilliam, this marked the first time he had specifically written a project with just one of the Python team. Not only that, he was potentially muscling in on an already established team, that of Palin and the *other* Terry. 'It was strange because Mike and Terry [J.] working together was not unlike Mike and Terry [G.] working together,' Gilliam says. 'Mike is a great tap dancer. He can do anything very easily, it bounces off him – words, characters – they come out very fast. But I also find that because of that ability he isn't as focussed as he could be. Both Terry [J.] and I are much more focussed, more monomaniacal. That's why I think Mike and Terry worked well together and why Mike and I worked well together; we balanced each other. Most of that dialogue is Mike's, though the ideas are mine. So whenever we started talking about "why does there have to be evil?", or Kevin has to "stay and carry on the fight," those things are all me.'

Palin found himself with less than two months to knock out a script, given a projected start of summer 1980. 'We plotted a rough story together,' Palin remembers. 'I think I probably helped him in suggesting areas in history where the boy should end up, then Terry would leave me to go and flesh out scenes, usually entrusting me to create the characters. But what actually happened to them, how they went through walls and all that, was more Terry's side.'

It was a working relationship that Palin enjoyed immensely. 'Of all the other Pythons that I've worked with, and I've done a bit of writing with John and I've done the odd piece with Eric Idle as well, and Graham, I found Terry Gilliam the easiest to work with. Perhaps it was because we weren't competing line by line. I've also got great respect for what Terry can produce on screen. It is usually breathtaking, and you know your writing is going to be used for something that is quite wonderful.'

The movie's already tight schedule became even tighter when a stage direction Gilliam and Palin had written was taken to heart by executive producer Dennis O'Brien. The direction read 'when the Greek Warrior removes his helmet he reveals himself to be none other than Sean Connery, or an actor of equal but cheaper stature.' It was, in part, meant as a joke. But with his eye on potential box office and foreign sales, O'Brien took the time to meet Connery on his own turf – a golf course. By the time they hit the nineteenth hole, Connery had signed, with the proviso that they fit him in during a few days break in May, before he was due to start filming Peter Hyams' *Outland*. Thus a fast-track project hit Formula 1 territory.

Filming for *Time Bandits* was due to begin in Morocco in May, but first a boy had to be found. Casting director Irene Lamb auditioned hundreds of kids for the central role of Kevin before settling on the relatively inexperienced Craig Warnock. 'Craig's brother was the one that was brought in to audition,' recalls Gilliam, 'and Craig came along with him. His brother was a real precocious, outgoing kid, but I kept watching Craig because Craig was quieter and seemed to be more sensitive and less showbizzy. It was wonderfully odd because he didn't really come for the part.'

By May, young Craig found himself with a skeleton crew acting opposite the 'man who would be King' and was indeed James Bond, somewhere in the Moroccan desert. Aware that everyone had been thrown in at the deep end, courtesy of his schedule, Connery was quick to step forward and help Gilliam in coaxing his young co-star. 'He suggested ways of shooting around the scene,' Gilliam recalls, 'to get his sequences done and then concentrate on Craig afterwards. He simplified it for me. He had just the right twinkle, the right amount of authority. Everything's there. We wanted a hero and Connery's a hero.'

As well as finding a Kevin, Gilliam also had to assemble half a dozen little people to play the titular Bandits. Needless to say, the dwarf casting directory is none too big in any country, and in England Gilliam found himself choosing from a limited, though thankfully highly talented, pool. David Rappaport had appeared on TV in *Not the 9 O'Clock News* and in Richard Lester's *Cuba* (with Sean Connery); Kenny Baker had been the man inside R2D2 in *Star Wars*; Jack Purvis was Baker's stage partner, one of the stars of the 'classic'

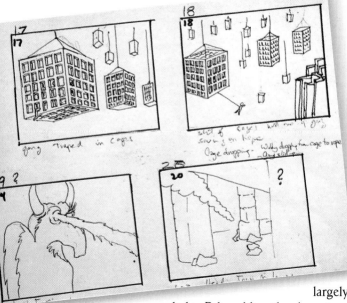

(Left and right) Original storyboard sketches for Time Bandits, 1980

Wombles movie, *Wombling Free* and Mike Edmonds, Malcolm Dixon and Tiny Ross rounded off the cast.

With Connery's scenes in the can, the now-expanded crew decamped back to Britain for filming at Lee International Studios in London's Wembley and on location in Hertfordshire, Gloucestershire, Essex and the West Country, as well as the water tank at Pinewood Studios.

Both Gilliam and Palin were keen not to overload the cast with star names, but O'Brien knew a certain amount of marquee value was needed to help sell the film. Thus, the role of Robin Hood, originally earmarked for Palin to play, was handed over to John Cleese, deemed a more bankable Python at that time, largely on the back of his hugely successful *Fawlty Towers*. This re-casting led to Palin adding the characters of Vincent and Pansy for himself and Shelley Duvall. When casting God, there was no surprise that Gilliam's first choice was a knight, Sir Ralph Richardson.

The future scenes in the original script had long since been abandoned, and budgetary restrictions led to the 'forest of hands' section being dropped before production began. One scene that was filmed and later cut involved two spider women.

'After they escape from the giant, they end up inside this cave and there are two spider women in there and they're knitting away. Everything is lacework and knitting, and what you see above them in all this spider webbing are these young knights in armour, all ensnared by these two old ladies who want boyfriends. They're in late Victorian/Edwardian wide skirts and you look down and you can see six little shoes. There they are, playing saxophone music and looking for boyfriends. It was a really, really funny scene,' describes the director.

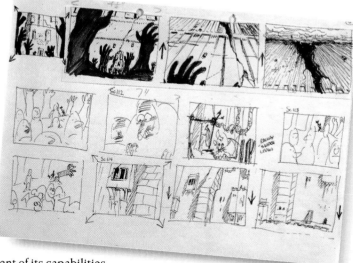

Gilliam had met rostrum cameraman Kent Houston, an associate of animator Bob Godfrey, back on *And Now for Something Completely Different*. Having made some money on *Holy Grail*, the filmmaker decided to invest in some optical equipment as a deal against tax, and together with Houston, he set up Peerless Camera. The company has created the optical effects for all of Gilliam's subsequent films. 'By the time of *Time Bandits* we had an optical printer,' says Houston, 'which was a beast that normally hadn't lived outside the film labs, and in England certainly was never really used to the full extent of its capabilities. The printer we got we bought as scrap, refurbished it, and then really drove it into the ground.'

Peerless Camera demonstrated its skills right from the start with the cosmic zoom that opens the movie. 'I took a toothbrush and splattered white paint on shiny black paper and that gives you stars,' says Gilliam, explaining this complex opening shot. 'The trick is to do a couple of layers of stars on different boards and splatter it first, then airbrush little glows around some of them. And then when you shoot them you just move in on both of them at different speeds and you start getting this shift between the stars. It's very tricky. Then I made some galaxies, again with airbrushing, and you just do several runs at the stuff on the rostrum camera and overlay them, and they all become this rich cosmos. It's as good as anything in *Star Wars*. The clouds again are airbrushed and superimposed,

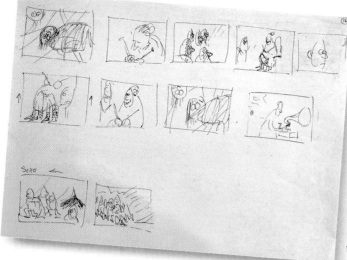

and the little village is an aerial shot I got from a picture library. We had to airbrush some of the buildings and put in these green fields. It was done very, very crudely and simply.' And of course very cheaply.

Similarly, the appearance of the Supreme Being as a disembodied head in Kevin's bedroom was another example of Gilliam improvising on the spot. 'I first did the Supreme Being as a full person,' the filmmaker says.

'The typical nineteenth century vision of God – a robe, beard, all that shit – floating in the air coming toward them. We had a guy do it and it kept looking awful. It didn't work. Then I realised it was the scale that was wrong; it didn't have any power because it was a full figure. So we took a big cardboard cut-out of a head, about four, five feet high. It was stuck on the end of a pole that was on the end of a dolly. We hoped there was enough smoke behind the thing to cover up the dolly. Then we pushed it at them, simple as that. In post-production I got an actor and put his head into a nineteenth century photographer's head brace and filmed it. Then we took each frame of film and blew it up to an 8-by-10 inch black and white thing, and put that under the rostrum camera and re-shot it, with the mouth moving. Then we had to line it up with the big cut-out head before sticking the two things together – and Bingo! it worked.'

'I think the worst job in the world has got to be being Terry's production designer,' offers Kent Houston. 'He is a true visionary and that extends to his visual effects. The great thing with him is that, unlike a lot of directors, he always gives us a brief, but he tends to change his mind as he goes.'

With filming rapidly drawing to a close, Gilliam was aware that he still didn't have an ending. Connery's tight schedule had left them unable to bring back Agamemnon, while once again, the paucity of budget had meant relocating the final battle against Evil in the Fortress of Ultimate Darkness. It was then that Gilliam remembered something Connery had said at their first meeting, suggesting that Agamemnon come back as the modern-day fireman who rescues Kevin from his blazing house at the end. Connery was due to be in England for one day to see his accountant, and stopped by the car park of Lee Studios to film two brief scenes as the fireman. The rest of this sequence was filmed on location several weeks later.

Gilliam was unhappy with many of Dennis O'Brien's decisions made during the post-production period on *Time Bandits*: 'He wanted *Snow White and the Seven Dwarves* and he wanted a whole lot of "heigh ho" songs in there, which we didn't do.' More specifically, O'Brien wanted to pepper the film with a number of new George Harrison songs. 'I threatened to put a nail through the film,' Gilliam laughs. 'I got him here and I showed him the nail and I said I'm gonna go right through the whole film. "I made it and I can destroy it" is what I said to him.' The

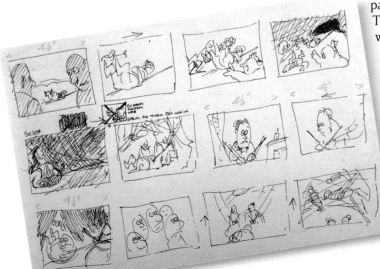

(Above) Katherine Helmond sensing something fishy. (Right) Agamemnon (Sean Connery) giving Kevin a ride through time

upshot of this conflict was that only one Harrison original was used, unobtrusively over the movie's end titles, and veteran percussionist Ray Cooper, who remains a valued friend and collaborator of Gilliam's to this day, was brought in to supervise the music.

Gilliam's doubts in O'Brien's abilities seemed to be borne out on the film's U.K. release in the summer of 1981. Despite strong reviews, the film failed to perform at the box office. 'The problem with Dennis is he didn't learn,' says Gilliam. 'He sold it like a Python film and he said "You can't refer to it as a children's film or a family film." It ended up not being a Python film and it never reached the kids' audience.'

O'Brien did however, redeem himself on the film's American release that November, traditionally a dead period at the U.S. box office. Having repositioned the film to appeal across the board, *Time Bandits* went on to become a huge hit in the States. At the time, a sequel was much in demand, but Gilliam refused: 'I just wanted to move on to the next thing. I wanted to use the success of *Time Bandits* to get *Brazil*, which nobody wanted to make, off the ground.'

BOB McCABE: At this point you seem fairly uninterested in adult characters, but more in fantasy characters and children.

TERRY GILLIAM: That was a very specific thing. What's nice about the genesis of the film is that it came from pragmatic choices. I wanted to show the film from a kid's point of view, but who's that height? Because I didn't think the kid could sustain interest from an audience's point of view, I decided to surround him with a gang of people who were the same height as he was. That's why the Time Bandits are that size, no other reason.

BM: How quickly did all that evolve?

TG: It was literally a weekend's work. I was sitting down and I couldn't get *Brazil* going. I had written about a hundred pages of *Brazil* at that point but it was going nowhere fast, and out of sheer frustration I just said, 'Fuck, I have to sit down and do a film that will get made and appeal to everybody.' That used to be the dream of studios — 'from eight to eighty.' So the first image was the horse coming out of the wardrobe. Then we had a boy and we want to see the world through his eyes. Then it goes into the flaws in creation and that God wasn't as all powerful as he says he is, and with just a week to get all the work done, you're going to make some mistakes. The next leap was these guys, who have been in heaven to be God's helpers, but that wasn't enough, what they really wanted was money.

Time Bandits was, in a sense, this frustrated leap back to childhood. I love the fact that greed was essential to the whole thing. It's back to material desires against pure desires. The kid's desires were pure. He just wanted to meet his heroes and they were all warriors, megalomaniacs basically, and to me the path of that boy is about learning that his heroes aren't as heroic as he thought they were. It's about losing faith in your idols.

BM: You were once quoted as saying 'Good is British, evil is American. There's no question about it.' But you didn't cast it that way.
TG: Why should I? Just because I think things like that? You disguise things. In all these things, I have these very hyperbolic ideas, but I don't neccessarily go that way. I always fudge it somehow, to confuse it. I try to let events involve themselves in the thing. I have a very clear idea of what I want and I go after it, but if I don't get it, I move on. So there's always the sense of using the events that are occurring around us, acquiescing to them. The film is not made by this megalomaniac who has got such a clear image and is going to make it that way or nothing. The main road to where I'm going is always very clear, but then I go these other ways because maybe it's more interesting to do that. But hopefully, at the editing stage, I can pull it all back and end up where I intended, even if I got there [by] a very different route and the place I got to has been changed by the way I got there.

BM: Were you aware of how much of a debt you owed to *The Wizard of Oz* making this? There are numerous elements — the bandits as munchkins obviously, but also the Supreme Being as Oz, time as the yellow brick road, and the dream structure of the movie, down to the dream characters appearing in the real world at end — Connery for Ray Bolger, and so forth.
TG: Yeah, I think I owe everything to *The Wizard of Oz*. The Supreme Being is Oz. When *Time Bandits* came out, the marketing people didn't want to show the little people because just before it, *Under the Rainbow* [set during the making of *The Wizard of Oz* and featuring Chevy Chase] had come out and been a disaster. And who did they blame? They blamed the little people. They said we couldn't show little people in the trailers, which is utter madness. So *The Wizard of Oz* is both our curse and our blessing. But it's right there, no question about it. I talk to other people, like Coppola and Lucas and Spielberg, and they all go back to *The Wizard of Oz*. And they would look at it and analyse it, and copy it. I would never do that. When I look at the way Lucas did *Star Wars*, I can see he's a copyist. He did his World War II film. Now there's nothing wrong with that, it's really good, but I want to rely on my memory of something. I want to make films that do that to people so that they all come away with their version of my film, not my version of my film.

BM: The *Thief of Baghdad* seems to be in there as well, in the impressive form of the giant.
TG: Again, the giant was another one where we went in the wrong direction at first. I was casting for the tallest guys I could find and we would get them and shoot them and very quickly we learned that the tall guys weren't what makes something look tall. I was using extremely wide-angle lenses to give that effect. So in the end we got a wrestler named Ian Muir who was incredibly squat, he was, like, square. But I got the camera down by his feet

(Above) Unseen shots of the Supreme Being appearing in Kevin's bedroom. (Below) The giant in actual size

with this wide-angle lens, then
that whole shape became the
right mass — massiveness is
all it was. Then we shot
him at four or five times
normal speed and had
him almost running,
so when it was
slowed down it
became a walking
speed. But as he's near-
ly running all those mus-
cles were   flapping, and I
think that does it. It became
a walk with such power in it.
Then in the water, when he's
coming up, to try and give a
little foam around the front,
we pumped out
condensed milk.

BM: There's a lot of disturbing
imagery and ideas in it,
particularly for a kids' movie.
TG: When we finished the film and
first started showing it, the adults had
some problems with it. They wanted to know
where they were, because the leaps were
really   disturbing to a lot of them. But kids
didn't have a problem, they went with the flow
of the thing. It was great. I was constantly being
surprised. To me, the most depressing thing about
getting older is that the surprises get less, things begin
to repeat themselves. I think the whole reason I'm making films is because of what films did to me, kicked
me into a direction I might not have gone or made me
look at life in a way that I wouldn't have.

BM: The movie celebrates the power of imagination
over reality, yet Kevin has some harsh lessons to learn
and he loses his parents.
TG: In all of them there are lessons to be learned. In
Jabberwocky you get the wrong fairy tale ending and
that's an awful lesson to learn. They're all didactic. It
isn't easy. I think it's a reaction against American films
where the learning experience is easy and things work

out well. I think it's much more ambivalent and uncertain. I think it's really painful. Then, at the end, he's left alone, which to me is the point — he has actually learned enough so he can stand on his own two feet. The line that I've always liked is when Fidget says 'Can he come with us?' and the Supreme Being goes, 'No, he's got to stay here and carry on the fight.' Now that's an incredible thing to say in a kids' movie like that, that it is a battle, that it is a fight, and it doesn't mean that good wins and bad loses. It's just a constant fight.

BM: How personal is his search for a surrogate father figure?
TG: That's a really intriguing one, because my dad was a carpenter, a really good guy. It's weird. You begin to think about where this comes from. I'm not sure if it's about parents or belief in something higher and the hope that there's something wiser and greater in control of this whole fucking thing. I think that's more what its about, and I don't know if it necessarily comes from good or bad parents. It comes from this other search, which has been going on for the millennia we've been around. I don't think it's just about your dad.

BM: Did you feel you were evolving as a writer as well as a director?
TG: The thing that was really hard were Sean Connery's scenes because we wanted them to be really simple and in the end they were the hardest to write. We had to keep cutting out all our ideas and reducing it all down to the little magic trick — which was Sean's idea. I think we learned something at that point because we're so used to trying to be entertaining all the time. We learned that you could actually be much more effective or moving on an emotional level just by being simple. You don't have to be a clever dick.

BM: You've said that you make these movies as a way to avoid growing up, and yet that's not what you're doing here. You're actually facing it in this movie and looking at it in quite an intense way.
TG: It doesn't mean you have to submit to it. It's just asking the questions and pondering these things. Someone's always said there's a melancholy in my stuff, and I think there is. On the one hand he's [Kevin's] growing up, but we don't want him to grow up. He's being taught the lessons and it's painful, and we know he is going to grow up at some point, but hopefully not too much. In the end it's always about loss. All the films are about loss. You don't get your dreams the way you want them, so it's either nostalgia, or melancholy, or loss, or things missed.

(Below) A Gilliam sketch of the giant's ship-hat (and left) the real thing. (Over) The Time Bandits caught, hanging in cages

Monty Python
Live at the Hollywood Bowl

AS EARLY AS 1970, the Pythons had started transferring their sketches — accompanied by some of Gilliam's animation — to the live stage. Their tours were never lengthy but always successful, culminating in their Drury Lane run in London and the City Center shows in New York.

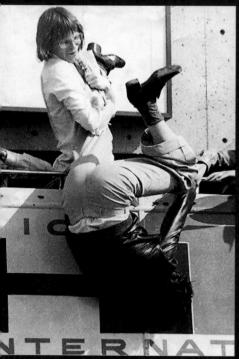

Terry Gilliam dangling Terry Jones over the edge of the stage at the Hollywood Bowl

'You'd be playing at City Center and people would be asking if the Beatles were in that night,' says Gilliam, recalling the rock and roll nature of the shows. 'I remember on the last night, there we were doing 'The Lumberjack Song', all dressed as Mounties, and in the group there was George Harrison and Harry Nilsson, all of us on stage doing it. Good times. I think all of us liked the idea of being a pop star in some way because if you were going to be anything in the late '60s, it was a pop star, and we got as close to that as comedians ever will.'

They got closer still in 1980 when, in a break between movie projects, the Monty Python team played a four-night stand at the 8,000 seat Hollywood Bowl. They were to receive the rather impressive sum of $1 million. 'But we didn't get it, because Denis O'Brien, our manager, took over and started doing it himself,' says Gilliam, 'and he made a complete hash of it.'

'It was great because it was a pop concert,' recalls Gilliam. '8,000 people out there and huge screens on either side, and people all in Gumby costumes. It's hard playing small places where you can see the faces. I found the whole experience slightly unreal, because we went out there to these huge roars of laughter and applause and stuff, and afterwards there was a big hospitality marquee with all of Hollywood turning up, so we were swarmed with all sorts of people.

'The thing I remember most is driving up in my car with all this heavy security in place. I'd drive through all the Nazis that were hired to protect us, park our car in the back, and go down to the little dressing rooms, where we'd piss around, then go onstage to these roars of applause and laughter, after which we'd have a little party and that was it. It's very strange. Driving up was almost the best thing. There's something about the back of the Hollywood Bowl and that sense of an impending event...'

In an attempt to recoup money lost on the concert, the group was forced to release the film *Monty Python Live at the Hollywood Bowl* two years later. The film was culled together from the four nights, presented in a different running order. It featured many classic sketches — the 'Parrot' sketch, 'The Lumberjack Song', 'Four Yorkshiremen', and so on — reflecting the 'greatest hits' nature of the whole affair.

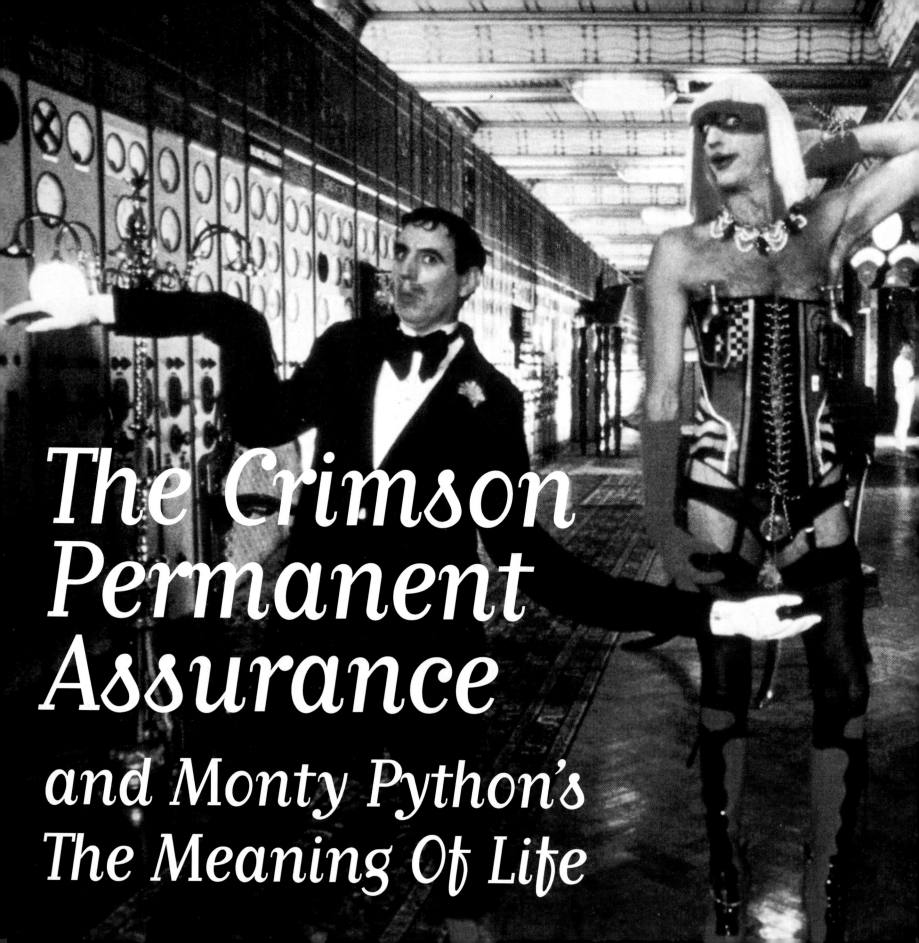

The Crimson
Permanent
Assurance

and Monty Python's
The Meaning Of Life

MONTY PYTHON'S THE MEANING OF LIFE BEGAN
as *Monty Python's World War III* and, briefly, *Monty Python's End of the World*. The latter was to have been set in the year 6000 AD and dealt with the last four minutes of life on earth; the former was conceived as a series of sketches on the theme of war.

A far more interesting idea, that similarly never came to fruition, was a movie based around a court case against the Pythons, with the team trying to prove that the film you were watching was actually a film and not a tax dodge. Scenes would be shown that were filmed on location in various tax havens, which then had to be defended by the team. As a means of financing the film, the Pythons were going to charge for commercials to be inserted directly into the film. 'I thought that was a brilliant idea for linking it all together,' says Gilliam. 'At the end we were going to be found guilty and killed.'

The project was having a hard time coming together, so as they had with *Life of Brian*, the team retreated to the sun, Jamaica this time, and tried to make some sense of the material they had so far assembled. 'There was one point in the writing,' Terry Jones said, 'where we all thought "This is it, we'll never do anything else again".' This proved not to be the case when Eric Idle hit on the title *Meaning of Life* over breakfast. 'The title was great,' says Gilliam, 'but we sort of ended up with the seven ages of man and it wasn't even that. I still love that other idea and I think we could have twisted and turned in more interesting ways than we did.'

With an $8 million budget, *Monty Python's The Meaning of Life* began shooting in 1982, and was in many respects the work of a more disparate group than before. The sketch format lent itself to the individual camps within Python dividing up the material, so the 'Every Sperm is Sacred' musical number is

clearly a Palin/Jones piece, for example, and the opening birth
section is clearly the work of Cleese/Chapman. 'Some of the
group had got spoiled,' Gilliam offers as explanation for the
working arrangement. 'They'd done some Hollywood films and
they wanted a more comfortable working atmosphere. I stayed
out of a lot of the main shooting. I'd turn up and do bits and pieces
along the way. I was feeling increasingly separate from them.'

For his contribution to the movie, Gilliam was keen to try
something experimental. *The Crimson Permanent Assurance* was
originally designed to fit in the middle of the film, under the
'Accounting' age of man. Conceived as an animated piece, Gilliam
decided to film it as live action, involving a number of complicated
effects and allowing him to experiment with model work, something
of a precursor to *Brazil*.

'It's really funny, I get this thing in my head that I don't want to
be an animator anymore. Once I moved into this other form of
thinking, i.e. story telling, longer stories, I didn't want to think about
these little bits of stuff.' Gilliam's animated contributions to *The
Meaning of Life* consisted of one scene involving a suicidal leaf, and
the opening titles, which in their use of vast filing cabinet images,
also touched on the ideas he was developing for *Brazil*.

The Crimson Permanent Assurance is a tale of aged accountants
who rebel against their American financial oppressors and set sail in
their Victorian building for the gleaming high rises of Wall Street.
The piece grew from a six-minute extract to a seventeen-minute
short that was eventually shown before the Python movie, as a
separate, albeit connected, film. 'I was testing things,' he recalls. 'I
pushed things that you could do in animation, but as live action.
The model work was really tricky, now it could easily be done on computers. All those reflective buildings were a nightmare, and because
of all the wide-angle lenses they were all tipped at different angles.'

Again, the imagery of the film prefigures *Brazil* at times, most
notably in the musty old office full of antiquated machinery and
rows of desks. Interestingly, if *Brazil* is Gilliam's oblique look at
corporate America, then *The Crimson Permanent Assurance* is a
more direct riposte. The American corporation that has taken over
this once family-run assurance company is clearly seen as the villain.
The directors are made to walk the plank or forcibly ejected from
multistorey windows (which Palin and Gilliam himself are briefly
seen to be cleaning). If America is seen to be co-opting the world,
then these olde-worlde, distinctly British, and even more fantastical
figures, are not going to let them. Once again imagination, and the
boyhood trappings of countless pirate movies, win the day over the
harsh, gleaming, yet soulless reality.

8
5A
MP 7 1 1 9
6
6A
KODAK SAFETY FILM 5063

MP 7 1 2 0
7
7A
KODAK SAFETY FILM 5063

MP 7 1 2 1
8
8A
KODAK SAFETY

4
11A
12
MP 7 1 2 6
12A
FILM 5063

13
MP 7 1 2 7
13A
KODAK SAFETY FILM 5063

14
MP 7 1 2 8
14A
KODAK SAFETY FILM 5063

17
18
MP 7 1 3 2
18A
KODAK SAFETY FILM 5063

19
MP 7 1 3 3
19A
KODAK SAFETY FILM 5063

20
MP 7 1 3 4
20A
KODAK SAFETY

2
MP 7 1 3 8

MP 7 1 3 9

MP 7 1 4 0

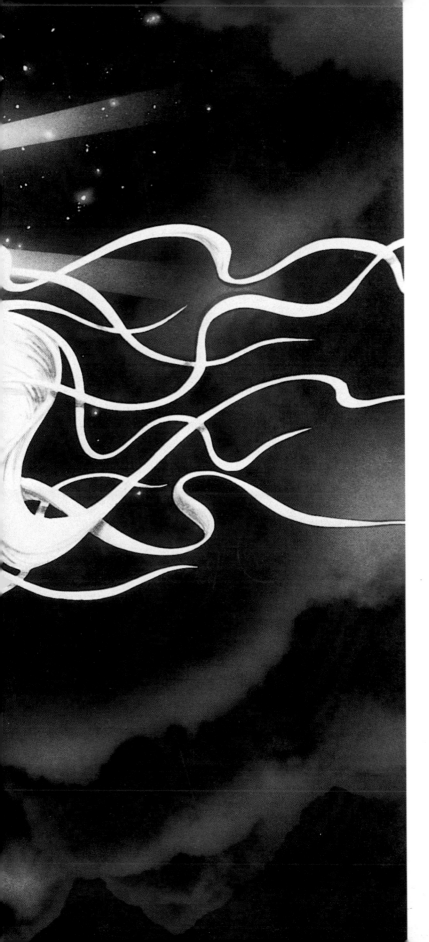

Both feature film and short were released in 1983 to healthy box office and critical acclaim, with the team picking up a special jury prize at that year's Cannes Film Festival. 'I felt it was over at *The Meaning of Life*,' says Gilliam. 'We all got to heaven, didn't we? That was really the end of Python as such.' The untimely death of Graham Chapman on 4 October 1989, the day before the twentieth anniversary of the first broadcast of Python, seemed to seal the fate of the team.

Fast forward to 1997. The remaining five members of the team met up in London to fire their management of several years. Eric Idle had an idea for a movie, involving a group of middle-aged medieval knights getting back together to go on one last crusade to the Holy Land. 'Now they've all made money, have their own families, and everything,' Gilliam elaborates, 'and they're trying to reassemble the group, which is good because it's dealing with the realities of our lives. We had a wonderful way of getting Graham in because we were going to bring along the Hallowed Bones, and they're gonna talk, because we had a lot of stuff from the albums we've done with Graham that was never used, so we were gonna have his voice in the box talking, occasionally.' Palin, Jones and Idle had hoped to begin writing some material later that year, but the screenplay never materialised.

In March of 1998, the Pythons regrouped again to appear on stage at the Aspen Comedy Festival. The plan was to discuss the movie again, but by the end of those three days, the film had been shelved and the possibility of a thirtieth anniversary tour for 1999 was on the cards. 'Mike [Palin] got pissed off because we discovered that John had actually announced this to some journalist before the meeting,' Gilliam remembers. 'And Mike said, "We've just been fucking manipulated. John's done it again. He's got his way." So Mike's reaction was "Hang on, I'm not gonna fall for that." There's a thing I find when I'm with the group – we all go back to being who we were when we were kids. The same relationships apply and I don't want to do that anymore. I don't want to do the tour and I told them. To me, we got out at the right time. We went out while we were still good and now we're a memory and I think a memory is quite a nice thing to be.

'I think, how many films have I got left? I've only got another, I reckon, fifteen years of decent filmmaking as a director. If I'm seventy two or seventy three and still able to make movies, that would be pretty extraordinary. But I'm not counting on it. So I'd like to get a couple of more films made, but we'll see...'

HAPPINESS

we're all in it together!

Hampstead's first $15 million community movie

aka Brazil

IT IS A GOOD THING THAT TERRY GILLIAM LIVES IN LONDON. Admittedly, it need not be London as such; it could be anywhere. But he wisely knows he should keep away from Hollywood. He needs the distance, as, inadvertently, his dealings with that industry town have served to expose the absurdities of the system. Gilliam's own notion that the stories surrounding his movies always somehow manage, for better or worse, to reflect, echo and exacerbate the stories within them, was never more true than during the next two films to follow *Meaning of Life*.

Both *Brazil* and *The Adventures of Baron Munchausen* remain two of the most influential movies of modern cinema, as much for what went on off-camera as on-screen. The first saw his critique on 'the system' stymied and nearly killed off by the system that had paid for its existence. The second saw a flight of fancy turn into a modern media tale of decadent excess. When examined in detail, *Munchausen* lays waste to the theory of the all-powerful *auteur*, becoming an almost tragi-comic vision of the production process as king-size screw up. *Brazil*, meanwhile, was an inspiringly heroic tale of one man against the machine. One might say that the Jabberwocky that was Universal Pictures was laid to waste by the Dennis that was Terry Gilliam. But ironically, *Brazil's* ultimate achievement was not to change the system but to publicise it. Gilliam's post-production battle with the monolithic Universal Pictures and MCA corporation made the stuff of movie boardrooms become the stuff of early evening news.

The fight that surrounded *Brazil* unexpectedly helped make the corporate side of movies sexy. Within just a couple of years, people could namecheck agents alongside their clients. A musical entitled 'Mike Ovitz — Superstar' was, without doubt, a missed opportunity. Today, just about every major newspaper in America, in its Monday morning edition, carries the box office top ten figures for the previous weekend. Where before audiences knew the price of a ticket, now a good few of them know the budget or how much the 'talent' picked up for the movie they sit, in the dark, popcorn in hand, to watch. If *Star Wars* changed the landscape of modern cinema, then *Brazil* significantly altered the paperwork. In keeping with the nature of the film itself, *Brazil* and the 'Battle of *Brazil*' (to which the film is always, and probably always will be, inextricably linked) was merely one cog that turned the wheel that drove the machine that produced the product, the result.

Brazil took its first breath on a beach in Port Talbot, South Wales, while Gilliam was shooting *Jabberwocky*. Many British beaches come complete with piers, fun fairs and illuminations. Port Talbot has a rather large steel works with a film of black soot that covers the sand.

(Left) A poster for use in Brazil.
(Below) The cover page for Gilliam's Brazil *script treatment*

Brazil

At night, with sporadic fire spraying from its towers, it looks a little like the skyline of *Blade Runner*. It is, in other words, a perfect place from which Terry Gilliam could draw inspiration.

'The sun was setting, the sky was beautiful and the waves were beautiful,' Gilliam recalls. 'I just saw an image of this guy sitting by the radio playing music and it wasn't 'Brazil' [the song], it was Ry Cooder playing 'Marie Elena', but it was a Latin love song, and it just got me. This idea of somebody living in a place that was so dark and dank and depressing, then this music you've never heard turns up on a radio station. You're off at that point. I think it's a result of having worked in advertising and coming to England and finding bureaucrats everywhere. All those frustrations of modern life that were slowly building up.'

This experience, coupled with a book on witchcraft trials of the sixteenth century that Terry Jones had lent him, which showed how those tried and tortured for witchcraft were obliged to pay for their own trial and incarceration, further fuelled Terry's imagination. 'So the idea of how you can work within an economically based system that tortures, and with all the paperwork taken care of, became incorporated into *Brazil*.'

Slowly Gilliam began to formulate his ideas, visions of a timeless world where minds were exercised by pushing paper, where the state left people in a state, where defiance took the form of acts of terrorism, but where the only truly defiant act lay in flights of the imagination. An early script bore the hand-written title 'The Ministry of Torture, or Brazil, or How I Learned to Live With the System – So Far, By T. Gilliam'. Trawling through Gilliam's ring-bound notebooks for the movie provides several alternative titles. One bears the Portuguese spelling 'Brasil' with a mirror reflection of 1984 beneath. At one point the filmmaker toyed with titling it *1984 ½* in homage to Fellini's *8 ½*. The phrase 'Retro Future – Viewing the Future Seen Through the Past' also appears in these early notes and scribbles.

Gilliam settled on the name *Brazil* early on. Despite the movie's themes of the intermingling of reality and fantasy, and Sam's eventual escape into insanity, the title was not a reference to the place 'where the nuts come from', but to the 1939 song by Arry Barroso that had now supplanted Ry Cooder in the director's head. 'It wasn't about the lyrics. But growing up in America in the 1940s, there was this sense that escaping to Rio, to South America, was the most romantic thing you could do, and that's the effect that song has on me. It's the idea of escape.' The director later once labelled his film 'Hampstead's first $15 million community movie,' in reference to the fact that many of those involved in the project (Gilliam, Jonathan Pryce, Michael Palin, Tom Stoppard and Charles McKeown) lived within spitting distance of each other in North London.

Gilliam began a first draft with his friend and *Jabberwocky* co-scripter Chuck Alverson. At this stage the character Buttle was called Timms and had no connection with Tuttle, the renegade heating engineer. Jill was still the Timms' upstairs neighbour, but was a childrens' social worker and no relation to Sam's fantasy figure, who turns out to be his Oedipally young-again mother (an idea touched upon in the final movie). There are also a great number of deleted fantasy sequences, such as those involving a landscape of moving eyeballs, flying eyeballs in which the characters travel at tremendous speed, a mile-long stone ship, and a gaping wall of eternal filing cabinets, into which Sam's winged incarnation must lie, coffin-like, to be filed away. The sectioning off and ultimate stealing of the sky also features in the original script, and the image of a grid-like sky, being removed piece by piece, first appeared in Gilliam's poster art for *Time Bandits* and has since been resurrected for a key sequence in the yet-to-be-produced *The Defective Detective*.

The obvious influence would seem to be George Orwell's *1984*. 'I never read *1984*,' Gilliam says with a touch of pride, 'but the thing that intrigues me about certain books is that you know them even though you've never read them. I guess the images are so archetypal.' Gilliam emphasised Franz Kafka as an influence over Orwell, referring to his movie as 'Walter Mitty meets Franz Kafka' and later amending this on the advice of a journalist to 'Frank Capra meets Franz Kafka'.

On screen the movie is described as taking place 'somewhere in the twentieth century.' However, early press reports set *Brazil* at Christmas 1984, the time of its original release date, once again emphasising the Orwellian links. By this point, *Brazil* was attaining a unique significance in Gilliam's canon of work. It was an almost cathartic outpouring of ideas, a nonconformist's view of conformity; a veritable documentary take on the world we rarely see around us; the cog in the machine spinning out of control for a running time of two hours and twenty four minutes.

The film was, of course, a hard sell. After the less-than-stellar box office performance of *Jabberwocky*, *Brazil* held all the allure of the proverbial fart in the proverbial spacesuit. So its creator proceeded with the time-pillaging dwarves and, somewhat unexpectedly, found himself a player in the town he had once called home. Hollywood wanted to know what the guy with the $40 million hit wanted to do next. What he wanted to do was *Brazil*; they offered him *Enemy Mine*. *Enemy Mine* was, to use the cliché of the day, 'this year's *Star Wars*', a science fiction movie that involved Dennis Quaid's all-American astronaut going head to, well, fish-head with Louis Gossett Jr in a rubber mask. Back then this was a hot project, so hot that, when Gilliam refused, people started to wonder what he could possibly be turning it down for.

In the meantime, Gilliam had met producer Arnon Milchan, a powerful European financier involved with Martin Scorsese's *King of Comedy* and Sergio Leone's *Once Upon a Time in America*, both projects starring Robert DeNiro. They two hit it off, Gilliam responding to Milchan's Hollywood-outsider status and buccaneering spirit. They talked about *Brazil*, and Milchan was sold.

Curiously, it wasn't until Gilliam had turned down *Enemy Mine* that financial backing began to materialise. 'We'd estimated a budget of $12 million and we were being turned down by everybody,' Gilliam remembers. 'Somehow having turned down *Enemy Mine* to do *Brazil* elevated *Brazil*, because for me to be asked to do *Enemy Mine* meant I'd been elevated to the top position, because this was going to be the biggest film that year. So all the stakes were being raised. It was like "top guy turns down film for other film? The other film must be really good." We were in Cannes [with *Monty Python's The Meaning of Life*] and because we were having no bites at $12 million, Arnon did the smart thing and we raised the price to $15 million. Suddenly, we were running round Cannes having a very funny time, and it ended up with a bidding war between Universal and 20th Century Fox, but we got the money.' As he had done with Dennis O'Brien back on *Time Bandits*, Gilliam used his Cannes hotel suite to act out *Brazil* for visiting Hollywood executives. 'All I do is make a lot of noise and they think they've got an action film,' he says.

20th Century Fox picked up the worldwide rights to *Brazil* for $6 million, while Universal held the domestic (U.S.) rights, paying $9 million of the total. Gilliam had financed his dream project, but he still wasn't happy with the script, knowing that the first draft with Alverson had many of the elements in place, but failed to capture the tone of what he intended. A friend suggested Tom Stoppard.

'I thought it would be a fantastic combination because he does verbal gymnastics the way I do visual gymnastics. We met and we liked each other, and I think the relationship was very intriguing because Tom's this great playwright, sophisticated, feted in all the great art circles of the world, and he really wanted to be a popular, much-loved person, like somebody from Monty Python, and I wanted the classiness of Tom Stoppard. It's very funny that we both seemed to fulfil something for the other. With Tom being a playwright, he'd always worked on his own. That's his style, so we worked that way and, ultimately, I found that frustrating. Some great stuff came out of that, but somewhere along the line I felt that the characters were probably too brittle. For example, Mike Palin's character was a real bastard, and he kept writing him as a bastard. I kept saying "No, he's got to be written as the nicest guy in the world; he's your buddy, he's got to be a sweet, sweet man".'

Stoppard wrote four drafts of *Brazil*. Amongst his numerous and significant contributions was

An evocative Brazil creation

finding a way to link Timms (now Buttle) with Tuttle, one of the movie's strongest story points, and one that brilliantly emphasised Gilliam's theme of a bureaucratic machine out of control, unable to deal with the reality of the people it should serve. Sadly, one of Stoppard's most ornate ideas never made it to the shooting script. Originally the movie began with a flying beetle in a forest. Soon the forest is completely laid to waste by a convoy of diggers and trucks. The beetle takes to the air and follows the trucks bearing the uprooted trees as they are pulped, turned into paper, and eventually printed into a document that arrives on the desk of a low-level bureaucrat. The document is on how to save the rain forest, and our low-level bureaucrat uses it to swat said beetle, dropping it into the machine (as in the finished film) that misprints the name Tuttle as Buttle, and thus sets the events of the movie in motion. It was an elaborate visual sequence that the film's budget simply did not allow for.

Ultimately, Gilliam grew frustrated with Stoppard's isolated approach to the writing process. He had been talking the project through with actor/writer Charles McKeown since the *Life of Brian* wrap party, and for the final draft they decided to put things on a more formal basis. 'Stoppard is somebody who likes to work on his own,' says McKeown, 'and Terry is much more collaborative. Although he liked a lot of the stuff Stoppard had done, the kind of feel of the thing had changed. They were in pre-production and the pressure was on, so my function at that stage was to reintroduce Terry to his own material.'

In the meantime, Gilliam was in Hollywood screen-testing just about every actress then considered to be bubbling under. A pre-*Top Gun* Kelly McGillis was in the running, as were Jamie Lee Curtis, Rebecca DeMornay, Roseanna Arquette and Madonna. Ellen Barkin all but had the role of Jill until the eleventh hour. Gilliam eventually cast Kim Greist. 'She was great in the screen test, but when I started shooting, it didn't happen,' the director admits.

Jonathan Pryce had originally met both Gilliam and Michael Palin when he was seated in front of them at a screening of Bernardo Bertolucci's *1900*, starring soon-to-be *Brazil* alumnus Robert DeNiro. 'I'd been on the box the night before in a half-hour comedy,' Pryce once recalled. 'He [Gilliam] said he liked my work. Then when he wrote the original *Brazil* he had me in mind to play the part [of Sam].'

But half a decade or more had passed since then, and Gilliam was determined that his Sam Lowry would be a young man of twenty two, twenty three years old. Aidan Quinn was in the running. Favourite at one point was American actor Peter Scolari, best known then – and now – as Tom Hanks' roommate on the cross-dressing sitcom *Bosom Buddies*. Rupert Everett, following his turn in *Another Country*, was an also-ran on this side of the pond, while another young actor, then just making a name for himself, was also keen. The name he was making was Tom Cruise.

'Tom Cruise wouldn't do a screen test,' explains Gilliam. 'It was really awful, he was practically in tears on the phone saying "I can't do it," and I said, "Well I can't consider you if you don't." I'd just seen a little bit of *Risky Business*, they were still cutting it, and I immediately thought he was great, but he wouldn't do a screen test. His people wouldn't let him. He was already managed at that point.'

Pryce, meanwhile, had just portrayed Martin Luther on TV and was subsequently looking overweight, over the hill and follicularly challenged. 'I read the script and thought there was absolutely no reason why I couldn't play the part,' said Pryce. 'The character didn't have to be twenty three he could just as easily be thirty three. So I phoned Terry and told him what I thought. I said "Test me... see how young you can make me look," secretly hoping that I'd do it well enough so that he and Arnon would say "OK. It doesn't matter even if he looks forty three".'

'We stuck one of Eric Idle's blonde wigs from Python on him,' recalls Gilliam, 'and screen-tested him, and I said, "Well that's it, he's got to do it, he's just amazing." I showed this to Arnon, who'd been seeing all these sharp young American guys, and here was this middle-aged guy with a paunch and an ill-fitting blonde wig, and Arnon said, "You're out of your mind." That was the only time we had a fight. I said "It's him or nothing," and that was the end of it.'

Arnon Milchan, fresh from *Once Upon a Time in America*, was instrumental in securing Robert DeNiro, although initially the actor was interested in the Jack Lint role, already earmarked for Michael Palin. With Palin having handed over his Robin Hood part to John Cleese on *Time Bandits*, Gilliam persuaded DeNiro to opt for another role, that of renegade repairman Tuttle.

'He'd never played a simple character like Tuttle before,' recalls Gilliam. 'I told him it would be very interesting to play a role without all the layers. And I think that frightened him at first, so I kept saying you're a plumber, but you're like a surgeon. So I think he made contact with a brain surgeon friend of his and he started watching brain surgery, just picking up all this surgical knowledge – he snaps on his gloves, all that stuff. Ironically the close-ups of his hands working are me, because we spent literally months on DeNiro's scenes, it was like doing a separate film. The props and costume departments were driven crazy by the amount of detail Bobby was into. However, when it came to doing close-ups, he was gone, so I had to put this costume on and it was so uncomfortable. It was like he had tied lead weights to his legs, back and hat, but it was what he needed to distract himself so he could do what he does. Actors are odd that way.'

Michael Palin, meanwhile, made the most of the role of friendly torturer Jack Lint: 'Both Terry and I like this idea of the baddie being a completely plausible, nice family man. In many ways *Brazil* was ahead of its time. Jack was a sort of 1980s character really, nicely turned out, belongs to all the right clubs, nice to his family, bought them presents, and was unbelievably cruel. It was partly based on a character Terry and I had met when we were in New York during the Pythons vs. ABC case, and we'd met somebody there who was a great defender of our material, but at the same time would do anything for the company. A really nice bloke who probably in the end would do you more damage than somebody who would come and punch you on the nose.'

Filming on *Brazil* began in November of 1983, with three weeks of location work at Marne la Vallee, a large post-modern apartment block in Paris, whose soulless streets and sleek design provided the base for Sam's apartment. Much of *Brazil*'s visual style comes from Gilliam's shrewd choice of locations, including the then underdeveloped London Docklands, which, in a disused power station cooling tower in the area, provided the director with the interrogation room that ultimately plays home to Sam. The film's key sets were constructed at Lee International Studios at Wembley, London, the old LWT studios where Gilliam had first started his television work on *We Have Ways of Making You Laugh*.

Working closely with production designer Norman Garwood, special-effects supervisor George Gibbs and art director John Beard, Gilliam had set about creating the unique world of *Brazil*, a possible future vision rooted in the past, or as Gilliam sometimes put it, 'the other side of now'. One of the key influences on the design of *Brazil*, and indeed on the movie as a whole, was Ridley Scott's *Blade Runner*.

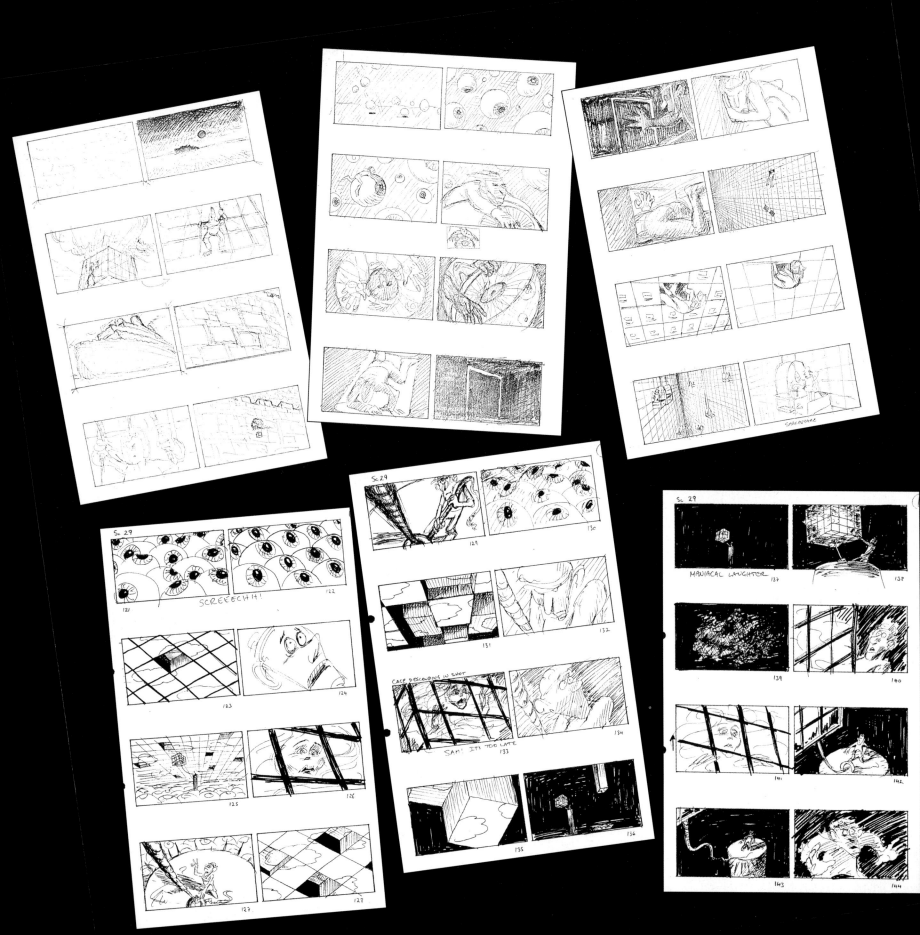

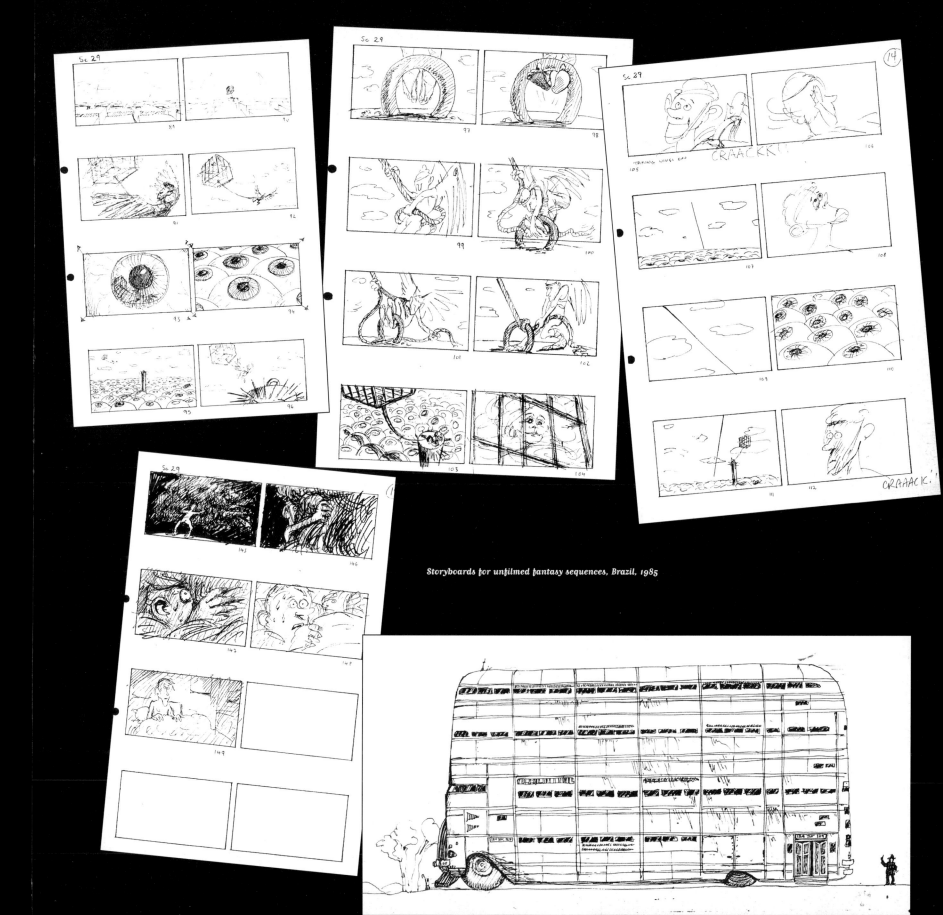

Storyboards for unfilmed fantasy sequences, *Brazil*, 1985

'I was trying to invent a technology,' Gilliam explains. 'Again it's a reaction against something, and I think I do it too often, but it was *Blade Runner* because *Blade Runner* really excited me, and then it really disappointed me. So I react against it. They had Syd Mead designing everything and so suddenly the big films all seemed to be designers, designers, designers. Everything was conceptual design. So we worked in a much more organic way just as a reaction against that. George Gibbs, the effects supervisor, got his hands on some old teletype machine and we got them for £25 each, so it was great. And they were all still in their housing, so I said, "Let's pull the housing off." That looked good, so I said, "Let's stick a television screen on there," and we got the smallest screen we could find, and got that out of its housing as well. And then we had to support that, so it was like sculpture with a whole gang of people participating in the making of the sculpture. Pretty much the whole film was done that way. And you end up with a look that you could never design because you can't think of it. It's not a single mind at work.'

Filming was due to finish in February of 1984. Gilliam was still shooting the following August. FX work, originally set to shoot in tandem with the main production, was proving too complicated, so was moved to the end of the schedule. Twelve weeks into production, Gilliam realised that his script was something of a behemoth, and likely to come in as a four-hour movie. Production was halted for two weeks while he and McKeown cut the script, removing the more elaborate fantasy sequences. 'In the original script the fantasy sequences were almost another film. So in the twelfth week I stopped and cut out a lot of pages, because what they were doing in the script, suddenly, we found with just an image on film we were achieving the same thing. So we didn't have to do it. Also, we couldn't afford to do it.'

The model work on *Brazil* remains one of its many highlights. Even by today's computer-generated standards, the flying sequences are hugely impressive. Somewhat appropriately, these scenes were shot in an unused building next to Lee Studios that was formerly Her Majesty's stationery supplies warehouse. Here vast tanks were constructed with a floor rail for the camera and a ceiling rig that supported the twelve-inch figure of flying Sam. Clouds took the form of a painted backdrop, some sculpted kapok and a constant supply of steam. As the figure 'flew' along the rail, battery-powered by a small motor in its chest, the camera would try to keep up, shooting at four (96 frames per second) or five (120 fps) times normal speed. The effect when projected at regular speed (24 fps) was a graceful, elegant flight that, to this day, has never been bettered on film.

Kent Houston and Peerless Camera were once again involved on the effects side, in particular the blue screen compositing in the flying sequences. 'Terry said to me, "What are the rules about blue screen?" And I said, "Nothing shiny, nothing blue, nothing out of focus, no loose hair, nothing translucent and no motion blur." And he went off and he did this shot of Sam and Jill flying, which starts off with her out of focus with her hair flying around, and Jonathan Pryce has got this shiny suit of armour on with blue stripes and he's got these enormous translucent wings which are sweeping around. She's got a translucent gown on. I saw this shot and nearly died. I thought if you can get everything wrong with a blue screen shot, this is it. We just had to find a way to deal with it.'

During this stage of shooting, the production suffered another setback – its director couldn't get out of bed. 'In the midst of all this we sold our house and moved into a council flat a friend had, and from there we moved into another house of some friends who were on holiday, so we were moving nomads around London. And at some point I just thought "it's never going to end." I don't know what happened, my brain just went catatonic. I couldn't get up. I couldn't move. I was in bed, catatonic.

'The doctor said, "There's nothing wrong." And I said, "If there's nothing wrong why can't I get up?" And he said "You're skiving." So I said, "No I'm not, I can't get up. I can't move." And literally for a week I was catatonic. We were into model shooting at that point, clouds and things, so [editor] Julian Doyle took over and kept shooting that stuff while I lay flat on my back. It was very bizarre. It was like a nervous breakdown of some sort. The whole thing had become so intense and so long-winded and so never-ending, and all of those things were happening. It was like a repeat of the summer camp *Alice in Wonderland* show that didn't happen. This has been like a recurring nightmare. And on *Brazil* I thought it might have been one of those things coming back to haunt me. And then, after five days flat, I just got up and said "Let's go. Let's get back to work".'

With filming finally completed, Gilliam enlisted the help of composer Michael Kamen. Gilliam's earlier films had been nominally scored, but music was integral to *Brazil*. It had been the initial inspiration for the film, which was now named for the song. Even some of the camera moves have the essence of a musical number about them, particularly the early dolly through the clerks' pool. Ray Cooper introduced the filmmaker to the composer. 'I had huge fights with him,' Gilliam laughs, 'because he didn't want to use *Brazil*. But it was really good, because Michael's scores are very dense, thick from top to bottom.'

'It remains practically my only major movie score that is about something,' says Kamen. 'This movie is about life as we live it. It's not a piece of entertainment, although it's very entertaining. It's a serious statement without being terribly serious, and this is what I think art aspires to. I never once used what we constantly rely on in Hollywood, which is a "click track," a device to keep the music exactly metrical and keep your timing straight. I gauged it all on the emotional content of a performance of a piece of music, and sometimes it didn't fit the film, and I had to do it again and try and make it fit.'

Brazil, which still came in under budget despite all the delays, opened in Europe in early 1985, unfortunately hot on the heels of Michael Radford's new version of Orwell's *1984*. Inevitably, the films were compared by critics and audiences alike. Surprisingly, some of the early critical responses to the film were very mixed, opinions that many reviewers seem to have recanted over the intervening years. Gilliam remembers that the 'Moment of the breakthrough feeling, when we knew we'd done something wonderful, was in Paris when we were doing promotions. It was at Christmas time and the press were coming forward and saying things like they just wanted to thank me for this wonderful gift. And they were saying it was poetry, and I was just "Oh fuck, this is great." The French were really the first to jump on it and get excited by it.' And, for once, the French were right.

Brazil is a densely packed, idea-laden explosion of visual and thematic invention. The tale of Sam Lowry, a man who knows his place in the system and conspires to remain beneath it – all the better to fuel his fantasies of beautifully distressed damsels and heroic winged saviours – explores more concepts in one film than you find in a year's worth of Hollywood products. It is probably Gilliam's most heartfelt film, another of his 'messages in a bottle' back to America that castigates convention and complacency, dissects and exposes the faults of the intricate machine we call society, and laments the horror of sacrificing dreams. The visual power of the movie complements these thematic concerns in often breathtaking ways. If anything, the movie is almost too densely packed, almost as if every piece of paper that explodes out of the Ministry at the end is another of Gilliam's thoughts, vying for attention.

It is a film of worlds within worlds, brilliantly conveyed in the opening shot: the frame of a television set pulls back through the frame of a window that violently explodes into the movie's neon title. Images exist within images; the fantasy of Sam's mind inside the reality of his life. It's not coincidence that the cogs in this wheel are all TV watchers. The only readers we see — the Buttles telling the story of *A Christmas Carol* – are the first to be punished.

If there was any doubt, the opening line 'Hi there. I'd like to talk to you about ducts' reminds the viewers that this is most definitely a Terry Gilliam film. The audacious ending, where the central character escapes into madness, could be the work of no other director. Certainly audiences agreed, with *Brazil* rapidly developing a loyal cult following and earning it a small profit at the European box office. Perhaps Michael Palin summed up its numerous charms best when he described *Brazil* as 'a movie so good, they named a country after it.'

The Americans, however, were less enthusiastic. During the film's production, the hierarchy at Universal Pictures had changed, leaving a man named Sidney J. Sheinberg in charge. Sheinberg wasn't sure of Gilliam. He doubted a man who called his production company PooPoo Pictures and whose letterhead featured a Hieronymus Bosch character with a spear up his behind. He doubted the 144 minute cut of *Brazil* even more. Sheinberg's principal objection was not just the film's length, but its tone, He wanted more of a romance, a happy ending even. In short, he simply didn't 'get' the movie on just about every level. Not surprisingly, a movie that viciously satirised bureaucracy had failed to raise a smile on the face of a bureaucrat. This became clear after the movie was first screened for the executives of Universal/MCA at the Alfred Hitchcock Theater at Universal Studios on 23 January 1985.

'I stood up in the projection box after the first screening for the executives, and I watched the backs of their heads and their necks were just knotted,' Gilliam remembers. 'And they all came out and Arnon was very excited. And I said "Actually I think we're in trouble". And then the trouble started. They tried to be reasonable. The worst thing in all of these cases is when you've finished a film, you're like a child. You're like a baby because you're totally defenceless, and you care about it and you know how flawed it is, and now you're being judged by all sorts of people. It's like you're in the headmaster's office and it's "You've been a very, very bad boy, Gilliam."

'And you walk into the studio and they don't really know what the answer is. They know they've got something they don't understand. And then it's warfare. It's awful because I'm in such a defensive mode because I feel so guilty. It was [Universal chairman] Frank Price who said, "You could end the movie when Sam finds Jill in his mother's bed and they could fly off in his dream." And I said, "Well that would be a Frank Price movie wouldn't it? Not a Terry Gilliam movie".'

The subsequent 'Battle of *Brazil*' continued until the following December. Gilliam initially agreed to cuts, reducing the film by eleven minutes. Still Sheinberg wasn't happy and threatened not to accept delivery of the film. As this would leave Milchan several million dollars out of pocket, Gilliam was persuaded by his producer to sign away his right to the final cut. This was what Sheinberg wanted and he promptly insisted on every foot of film being shipped to Los Angeles, where his team of editors set to work on cutting the movie by a third, upping the romance and completely castrating it with a happy ending. This cut later played as the American TV version of the movie.

Gilliam, meanwhile, tried desperately to save his film. A planned student

screening at the (appropriately named) Arthur Knight's Film Symposium, at the University of Southern California, was cancelled mere minutes before curtains up at the insistence of Universal's lawyers. Gilliam sought to involve Sheinberg protégé Steven Spielberg by screening the film for him. Spielberg loved the movie, but played no part in swaying his mentor. Plans to bus critics across the border to see the movie in Tijuana were also abandoned.

Eventually, Gilliam decided to take the whole thing public by placing a one-page advert in trade bible *Variety*, reading: 'Dear Sid Sheinberg, When are you going to release my movie, *Brazil*? Terry Gilliam.' The ad was enough to turn the conflict into a global news story, a David and Goliath tale of the little filmmaker taking on the might of the biggest studio in town. The image of the tiny wingless Sam faced with the giant marauding samurai of his dreams was more than appropriate. 'Terry quite likes that situation,' explains Michael Palin. 'He thrives on some form of opposition. If people just said "Thank you Terry, that's wonderful," he'd be very unhappy. He's got to have some wall out there that he's got to climb or kick his way through.'

Helping Gilliam kick through that wall was the usually reluctant Robert DeNiro, whom the director persuaded to make two morning chat show appearances in defence of the film they had made, not the one Universal were still in the process of unmaking. 'I went on the Maria Shriver show,' says Gilliam, 'and she said "I hear you have a problem with the studio." I said, "I don't have a problem with the studio. I have a problem with just one man, and he looks like this." And I pulled out a picture of Sid.'

Arnon Milchan eventually organised some clandestine screenings for the Los Angeles Film Critics in December of 1985, almost a year after the first screening. They responded by awarding *Brazil*, an unreleased film, Best Film, Best Screenplay and Best Director. Gilliam had just come back from watching *Back to the Future* when he heard the news. With no other avenue available to them, Universal released the 133 minute American cut of the movie for an Academy Award-qualifying week that same month. The film later reaped two Oscar nominations: Best Screenplay and Best Art Direction. However, when finally released nationwide in February of 1986, it failed to set the box office on fire, in part due to Universal's half-hearted commitment to promoting it.

Nevertheless, Gilliam had won. His film was out there for all to see. At the time he was rather pleased with himself. 'You can only rub somebody's nose in it so much,' he told the *Daily Mail* when he heard of his triumph. 'I've dragged a faceless figure out into the open. His own words have condemned him. Besides, I actually like Sid and I think he likes me.' A surprisingly optimistic comment from the man who made *Brazil*.

'It allowed me to get out of my system something that has been bothering me for a long time,' Gilliam elaborated at the time, 'the frustrations of living in the second half of the twentieth century. Life appears to be richer, but it's just becoming more difficult to control. *Brazil* had become the focus for a lot of energy that has been building up in the States against the approach to filmmaking, that it should follow an easily defined proven formula. I've broken the categorisations and been vindicated.'

BOB McCABE: Many regard *Brazil* as the definitive Terry Gilliam movie. Do you think it's your best work?

TERRY GILLIAM: I have no idea. It was probably the most personal, cathartic one: the one I had to get out of my system, the one that involved more things that made me angry. People talk about it more than anything else. It's the one that seems to have hit people who like films, and people who make noise, more strongly than the other films. I watched it a few years ago in Paris, and it was strange because I was watching something I hadn't done. An earlier version of me had done it. And it was really good but it wasn't as good as everybody told me it was going to be. It's strange. I don't know what it is about *Brazil*. It's the sense of

THEY TOIL THAT WE MAY DREAM

what it's about that's probably the important thing. At the time the reviews were very mixed, to say the least. People thought it was overly self-indulgent, that it was just this visual cacophony, there was no character in it. The reviews didn't even mention Jonathan Pryce — they were too busy talking about the design and the look of the thing. Obviously I created a world there and an atmosphere that nobody else had done, but to me it was just carrying on from German expressionism and *Metropolis* and *Caligari*, and all of that stuff. And trying to do what *Blade Runner* didn't do because it sold out in the end. The ending of *Brazil* is very much a reaction to *Blade Runner* because the ending of *Blade Runner* I hate. It was a wonderful film and built my expectations and then has this appalling ending of driving off into the sunset.

BM: There's a constant in your scripts it seems, that the finished movie is in there somewhere struggling to get out of this bigger, more unwieldy thing.

TG: You work on the script and you make the script as good as a script can be. Then you start making it and reality starts pushing its face into the thing and certain things you can't do, new ideas come up. As you bring everybody into the process, from designers, costume people, actors, everything starts changing. You look for locations, you can't find what you wanted but you find something else. For example, the final interrogation room in the script is a forty foot cube, all with white tiles, because the whole design of the film was going more and more rectilinear, more into a grid, more into a cage, so it ended up a perfect cube. Well, we were down at Croydon power station looking for things and I'd always wanted to look inside one of those cooling towers, and I poked my nose in and went 'fuck, that's it.' So having written and been very clear about one's intentions, I threw them all out the window because I found something that interested me more. It's a whim, but the whims are based upon me feeling I'm so imbued with what the film is about that my choices are true to the spirit of the thing. So I become the spirit of the thing, I suppose, and I've got to be that.

BM: So is the film you end up with better than the blueprint?

TG: It doesn't feel that way at the time. In retrospect I can justify anything. I can live with it. And I have the ability to confuse the final thing with what I intended. But when I look back at some of the scripts I say 'Shit I missed that.' It's never as good as you imagine. The film is just what it is. It's better in some parts, worse in others. All it does is continually remind me of how little I know about making films, and certainly about writing scripts. It's a weird process, but I like it because at every stage of the thing, it's being made. It isn't a script and then a film. The whole thing is totally organic. It's what the films are all about: imagination and reality. The imagination is the script we've written, and reality is the making of the thing, and there's this battle that goes on between them. But I think it's the final editing, when you're making the final choices of what you can live with and what you can't, what's in, what's out, what you can fix and what you can't, that defines it ultimately. And that's where a lot of films go wrong. At the very last minute you can fuck up all your work. And the pressure from the studio and all these people around you is all designed to make you make that mistake. And you don't know who to trust. That's what happened on *Blade Runner*, because *Brazil* and *Blade Runner* relate a lot, and Ridley — whatever word you want to use — he fucked it. He sold out, he put the wrong ending on the film. Whether it ever had a right ending, I don't know, but it wasn't that one.

BM: Nearly all the contemporary reviews thought the movie was set in the future. It was taken as a future vision.

TG: I kept saying it takes place everywhere in the twentieth century. It's all the stuff around us, it's just been twisted. The clothes are 1940s, 1950s. The car he drives is a Messerschmidt. That's what's intriguing; it's like Fellini. I thought Fellini was a great fantasist, but you go to Rome and you realise he's a documentary filmmaker. But he saw it first in a sense. Other people didn't see Rome like that, but it was there. Well I selected enough bits of life that the composite seems to be something new, but it's just the shit that's around us.

BM: There are many autobiographical elements to the movie. You once described the L.A. police riots you witnessed as 'the first nightmare I ever experienced in reality,' which in many ways defines the essence of *Brazil*.

TG: The police brutality in the film is very much from that. It's one of those things when you just wake up one day and you go, 'So this is what it's like to be black, or a minority, and the cops are not nice people.' And that brutality was in there. The arrest at the beginning [of Buttle] was supposed to be really ugly. On the one hand it's exciting because they're crashing through the door like they do in movies. But it was just awful. I really went out of my way to try and shock people. I kept saying it was cinematic rape. I got them in there and I was violating them. I really wanted to shock people and just push it. One side of me thinks this is really juvenile, this always wanting to push further, just showing off.

BM: Dr. Chapman's acid technique, I believe, stems from an incident with your father.

TG: He had little bits of skin cancer. And normally they'd just cut it off, but he'd been advised to go to this acid man, basically. There was a bit on his ear and you could just go to this guy's practice and it could be done on the spot. So he applies his acid, puts a compress on it, bandages it and says 'Go out and sit in the park for an hour'. So my dad goes out and sits with my mother and the acid started leaking down and he was in terrible pain. And my dad was always very stoic. My parents were always the kind who, if a doctor said do it, they'd do it, because they had that awful stoic belief in professionals being good. So he's in terrible pain but he does what he's told, and he comes back in and they take the compress off and his ear's been burned away. All that was left was the rim, the whole centre of the ear was gone. He just sat

HELP
The Ministry of Information
HELP YOU

there. He had plastic surgery to put the rest back in and they went to sue, because the guy had been doing this to several other people. Unfortunately my dad died before the suit had been taken care of. So that was very personal about the acid man.

BM: Sam should be the hero of the piece but he isn't. He's far too weak to begin with, and then when he does do something, it's all completely selfish. Didn't you worry about the sympathy factor?

TG: I didn't in a sense. He's the guilty party. He is the system. He is what goes on. He's been living in this little sheltered world. He's an outrageous character. He's got all the privileges through his father and other's connections. He's bright so he should be taking responsibility in that organisation, but he shuns responsibility. He lives in his little fantasy world. Then he goes out and delivers the cheque to Mrs Buttle because it's Christmas; it's his good deed. He really feels like he's a good guy and he's going out to do something that nobody else will do. And BAM! he gets shat upon by this woman and he can't understand it. And then he finds his fantasy and he does become more human and becoming more human does make him more vulnerable. But ultimately he's being punished for his guilt of all those years of being one cog in the machine that just kept the machine going. And at the end he blows up the Ministry but it's all fantasy. It's a bit too late in the day. The real hero of the piece is Tuttle because he's the guy who goes out there and makes things work. So he becomes an embarrassment to the system, which is all based on inefficiency. And he's American you notice. But Sam is so pathetic. His view of reality is really fucked. I think he's a really modern character. He's a totally modern man.

BM: The first pan through the clerk pool is staged like a musical number.

TG: That's what started happening. There's that moment and there's the moment with Warren running round with all his boys behind him — we didn't have the music on those scenes at first. But it was like hearing music in my head when I did it. There's a side of me that wants to do a musical and play with the camera moves. But in this case the camera move for me was very much like [Kubrick's] *Paths of Glory*, running through the trenches. And that's how I wrote it, right from the beginning, as this huge camera move, a push through. And I think when we're doing those shots, I can hear music in my head. It was really a hard shot to do, because you've got such wide-angle lenses, and trying to get people close enough to the camera was just really hard. The first part of the shot is pulling back and then the second half is moving forward. But I don't think we did more than eight takes.

BM: You have a dwarf in one scene. Did you not feel confident enough to make a film without a dwarf?

TG: No, no. I need somebody I'm taller than. It was Jack Purvis again, and I was just trying to find a part for him.

BM: Were any of the deleted scenes actually shot?

TG: We shot some tests of the eyeball landscape. We had the eyeballs all made up. They could all move, but the trick was trying to get them to all turn at the same time looking in the one direction. That's the kind of thing you could do really easily now with a computer, but we built it and shot tests and I still wasn't quite happy and it kind of went. And I think I brought the hand forest [excised from *Time Bandits*] back in for this one. This stuff never goes away. And the mile-long stone ship, that's a great image. It was huge inside. It was all about capturing the day. What happens in these fantasy sequences was he's out there trying to get Jill and he's trying to escape from the evil forces, and the whole sky, the day, the light is stolen and it's blackness everywhere. That's something I've saved for *The Defective Detective*.

BM: When you'd finished *Brazil* and before all the fighting began, how happy were you with it?

TG: I thought it was great. It had already been released in Europe before all the battle started. It always comes down to the very simple thing that my name is on it so I've got to be happy with it. If they want to put their name on it, fine, they can do what they want. But if you're going to put your name on it, you've got to take responsibility for it. And you've got to feel, for better or worse, this is what you have done. Every movie for me is the first and last movie I will ever make. So if it goes badly, it's really depressing.

BM: Did you enjoy the fight at the time in any way?

TG: No. It's more enjoyable than lying down and taking it, is all I know. On the one hand I thought we were doomed, but on the other hand I thought we're just gonna go for it. And at least I can keep my adrenaline going when I'm like that. I enjoyed the sheer ridiculousness of Sid Sheinberg and his inability not to put his foot in his mouth. And as long as we could maintain a certain merry prankster approach to the thing and keep it funny. Driving him crazy was the only pleasure I was getting out of it because he was driving me crazy. The idea of trying to personalise a corporation was important to me because it was everything about *Brazil*. In some awful way I'm glad it all happened. It's like people talking about having been in a war. People always say it was the best years of their lives. And at the time it doesn't feel that way, but looking back you were really alive and exhilarated, thinking fast, being clever.

BM: Did you ever have the fear that should come with that? For example, taking the advert in *Variety* could very well have led to a case of 'you'll never work in this town again'.

TG: When the idea came up, I just decided to leap in and do it. And the minute I got my *Variety* and opened it and saw it, that was the moment. I just went, 'Oh fuck, what have I done. Oh shit, oh no.' And that lasted about five minutes and then it was, 'OK, it's done.'

BM: How political a move on your part was it to screen the movie for Spielberg?

TG: He was Sheinberg's protégé, and I knew Steven and I said, 'come and look at it, is it too long?' And we went over to Amblin and just he and I watched it and at the end I asked him, 'How long is it?' And without looking at his watch, he said 93 minutes. I said 'No, it was two hours and twenty four minutes — it's not too long is it?' But I don't think he did anything to help. You know, he's both very, very clever, but also a kid who just sees something and grabs it like a magpie. So one of the things that came out of it, I'm convinced, is next morning he's shooting second unit for *Back to the Future*. And in the beginning of *Back to the Future* you see Michael J. Fox wandering into the Doc's place and you see all the machinery that's doing just what the machinery does in *Brazil* when Sam wakes up in the morning. And I don't think that was in that film originally. I think Steven bagged it from us and *Back to the Future* came out before us because of the fight. I remember somebody called up and said 'Have you seen *Back to the Future*?' I said, 'No, why?' They said 'The opening. It's a direct steal from Jonathan waking up.' And you don't see the actor in there, it's a second unit shot.

BM: Do you think that ultimately it was an industry-changing event, or just two personalities clashing?

TG: I don't think it changed the industry. It was a glitch. I wasn't part of the system. And it was a very unique situation. I had enough of a reputation from *Time Bandits*. So it wasn't like I was a small independent filmmaker who could easily be dismissed to the art houses. I had done a big commercial film. But I had no connections in Hollywood. I now have more connections in Hollywood so it's harder to have these fights, because there's too many people trying to make sure we don't have those kinds of fights. I wish there would be more of these things, just to keep it stirred up, just to keep people thinking. But it doesn't happen. And I think it required a real naïveté on my part, and madness. You have to be crazy to do this. And I think for a moment it did something, but it didn't change anything ultimately. In a way it did become about two personalities, but they represented two sides and a whole way of thinking. Sid's was the perfect corporate view, and I really think he thought if I won this one the floodgates would be open and there'd be chaos reigning in Hollywood. He's a very conservative man. He's not a bad guy, it's just his view of the system and the way it works is very conservative and establishment.

The most disappointing thing was Ridley Scott. Before it was resolved there was a big thing in the *Sunday Times* on *Legend*, in which he talked about how valuable it was to collaborate with the studios. I read that as saying that people like Gilliam are assholes and bastards. And then *Legend* came out and fell flat on its face, and Ridley had basically abandoned Arnon Milchan and gone off with Sid Sheinberg, yet after *Legend* opened he couldn't get Sid on the phone.

A Terry Gilliam end-of-shoot sketch

The Adventures of
Baron Munchausen

'I GET THE FEELING THAT, a bit like *Brazil*, the making of the film is going to be like the film itself. Where *Brazil* was about a nightmare, this one is about impossibility and overcoming it.'

So Terry Gilliam told *Sight & Sound* magazine as he prepared to shoot *The Adventures of Baron Munchausen*, his fourth film as sole director. It was, naturally, a hell of an understatement. There's a feeling of grand folly about *Munchausen*, but then there should be. Here we have a visionary filmmaker translating somebody else's tales to the screen, on a scale that the budget was in no way able to accommodate, working with a producer who was overly busy posing in his boxing gear and bragging to Hollywood about the way he had sabotaged the set to help production costs. In addition, there was an international crew who couldn't talk to each other without interpreters, who were filming in the biggest studio in Europe that was missing part of its roof. Moreover, the crew brought a hitherto unknown amount of special effects to that studio which had little or no effects technology. The film was backed by an American company that was busy sacking the British guy who sanctioned the project in an extremely public manner. Then there was a proposed cast of thousands, battle scenes on an epic scale, and various Italian technicians who would rather take a few extra sharp suits on location than the principal costumes required for filming. Not to mention the overpriced, dubiously trained dogs, horses and elephants. If, as Gilliam suggests, the stories about the making of his movies could practically be movies in their own right, then the making of *Baron Munchausen* would be one of those travelogue Euro-farces from the 1960s, complete with a rent-a-face all-star cast and a Blake Edwards sensibility.

Ray Cooper first introduced Terry Gilliam to the Baron, courtesy of a copy of *Baron Munchausen's Narrative of His Marvellous Travels and Campaigns in Russia* by Rudolf Erich Raspe. The book was a collection of seventeen tall tales believed to have been told by the real Baron von Munchausen, a former military man, who became known as a great spinner of outlandish yarns in his native Germany in the mid-eighteenth century. Raspe's story and its illustrations by Gustave Doré captivated Gilliam. George Harrison had also pushed the filmmaker in the direction of the Baron, but by now Handmade Films were folding and Gilliam had set up Prominent Features in Camden, London. Designed as a studio complex to accommodate both himself and the other Pythons, *Munchausen* was set to become the first movie produced under this banner.

Gilliam jokingly referred to *Munchausen* as the 'fourth part of my trilogy', and the film was clearly related to its two predecessors. *Time Bandits* saw a young boy dream his way through space and time; *Brazil* saw that boy grown up and escaping the harshness of his day-to-day life by retreating into the insanity of a world of his own making. *Baron*

Munchausen was the tale of a storyteller left old and weary by his battle against the Age of Reason. It was with this film, and for the first time in any of Gilliam's movies, that finally fantasy triumphed over the so-called real world.

The first draft of the screenplay was written by Gilliam and Charles McKeown during 1985, while the battle of *Brazil* was still at its height. In light of that, it is no wonder that the character of the Right Ordinary Horatio Jackson (played in the movie by *Brazil*'s Jonathan Pryce) was, on release, seen by many as a thinly-veiled Sid Sheinberg, especially when mouthing such dialogue as the prophetic, 'He won't get far on hot air and fantasy'.

But the most telling aspect in the writing of *Munchausen* is not the triumph of its ending, but the resigned tragedy of its hero. While Gilliam was struggling to see his previous film released in the U.S., he was penning lines for his next lead figure (as before, a variant on Gilliam himself) which spoke of failure and resignation. 'There's no place for *Baron Munchausen* in the modern world,' the character said in this first draft, 'where everything's analysed, quantified, measured, rationalised. It's not for me... I'm old and tired and sick of not being believed.'

This early draft of 138 pages, which bore the title *The Impossible Adventures of Baron Munchausen*, was completed in November 1985. 'The feel of the thing was there in the first draft,' says co-writer Charles McKeown. 'And that theme of Terry's, of the Age of Reason and the destruction of the imagination by the bureaucratic, which I suppose is a theme that comes from *Brazil* to some extent.'

Arnon Milchan was originally in the frame to produce *Munchausen*, but during the *Brazil* battle the relationship between producer and director had changed for the worse. In September 1986, on the Lake Como location of his film *Man on Fire*, Milchan introduced Gilliam to Thomas Schuhly. Schuhly, a former collaborator of German *auteur* Rainer Werner Fassbinder, was riding high on the recent success of his production of Umberto Eco's *The Name of the Rose*, starring Sean Connery. He was eager to forge a relationship with Gilliam and offered to bring Gilliam and the *Baron* to Cinecitta studios in Rome, home to one of Gilliam's favourite filmmakers, Fellini. The fact that Schuhly was commonly known as the self-styled Rambo of German filmmaking should have set alarms bells ringing for Gilliam, but it didn't.

'I liked Thomas because he was very smart, mad, full of energy and convinced we could do it,' says the film-maker in retrospect. 'It was a wonderful period of people fooling each other, and themselves, because Thomas was the executive producer on *Name of the Rose* and Jake Eberts was executive producer on it, too. So there was a meeting in Jake's office between the three of us, and Jake thought Thomas was OK because he was with me, and I thought Jake was OK because he was with Thomas, but they had never met. Everybody was fooling each other, and we walked into this thing and off we went on this romp.'

Oscar-winning British producer David Puttnam had recently been enshrined as head of Columbia Pictures in Hollywood. He arrived with a very public mandate to shake up the U.S. industry by cutting salaries and budgets and concentrating on quality productions over box office pap. Now, over a decade after his arrival, Puttnam's impact on that town has still not been felt. Gilliam asked him for $20 million to make *Munchausen*, a figure far in excess of what Puttnam had planned to spend. However, Puttnam's right-hand man David Picker loved the project, and soon Columbia agreed to pick up a certain amount of the film's costs in exchange for various distribution rights. Schuhly raised the remainder of the movie's proposed

(Below) Production sketch by Dante Ferretti

$23.5 million budget by selling ancillary rights to other countries.

'It was very chaotic,' says Gilliam, 'but that kind of madness required the kind of madness that Thomas had. He really wasn't experienced enough, but his heroes were Alexander the Great, Napoleon and Dino DeLaurentis.'

Schuhly's budget apparently exemplified 'that kind of madness', because anyone else who had looked at McKeown and Gilliam's screenplay would have known there was no way it could be realised for $23.5 million. 'The first budget came in at $60 million,' Gilliam recalls, 'and Thomas fired the guy. The next one came in at $40 million, and he was fired too. The next one came in at $30 million, same thing. The last one came in at $23.5 million and he was the guy who got the job.'

The production was now up and running, with casting underway. Eric Idle was on board as the Baron's servant Berthold, Sean Connery was pencilled in for another *Time Bandits*-like cameo (as the King of the Moon) and Marlon Brando was in line for the role of the god Vulcan.

'One of the best things about making the film is that I got to spend an afternoon with Brando,' recalls Gilliam. 'There was a lot of foreplay going on there that was really leading nowhere. I actually told Thomas it was no good offering him a lot of money. At that time Brando was still very keen on Native American Indian rights, so I told him to say, "Marlon, you work for free and the money we pay you will go directly to the Indians, it won't touch your hands." Thomas would never do that, but I thought it would be the only way to get him, to call his bluff, and he'd react to that because he'd know that you were being smart.'

Brando bailed out and PooPoo Pictures found themselves visited by the vice squad – adverts asking for young girls to audition for a role in the film, complete with the Bosch-inspired PooPoo logo, were thought to be the work of a paedophile ring. Eventually Canadian Sarah Polley landed the role of Sally.

Gilliam had more trouble casting the Baron himself. 'My first choice actually was Peter O'Toole, but then I got more and more obsessed with finding somebody, the same way I did with Kim Greist in *Brazil*, whom nobody knew. He was just the Baron and he didn't exist in any other form. So I started looking for a star that nobody knew, and John Neville was the only one who fitted that bill. Neville first made his name doing *Alfie* on stage, before Michael Caine did the film. We approached his agent, who said he didn't do films, and then at the very last moment our make-up lady, Pam Meager, asked if we'd ever thought of John Neville. I said, "Yeah, but he doesn't do films." But Pam knew his daughter so we called her. John turned out to be a big Python fan. We went off to Canada where I met him, and Bingo!'

One of the biggest incentives for working with Schuhly was the lure of filming in Rome. Not only had the producer promised it would be cheaper, but Gilliam fell in love with the idea of filming in Fellini's workplace alongside fabled designer Dante Ferretti and cameraman Giuseppe 'Peppino' Rotunno. As he explained to the *Village Voice*, Ferretti had been greatly impressed with the look of *Brazil*: 'I absolutely wanted to do a picture with Terry Gilliam and two weeks later he called me, as though he had been invoked.'

Filming was scheduled to begin at Cinecitta on 7 September, but didn't. This was largely due to a lack of completed costumes, finished props or, indeed, a set. Eric Idle, shaven-headed for his role as Berthold, took the delay in his stride, as he recalled to journalist and author Andrew Yule: 'I got home to this empty villa, completely bald and alone, with no food in the house. It was a choice of either going out for a meal or ending it all. I decided to brass it out and hit the streets of Frascati. People backed off as I walked along, thinking I'd escaped from a mental institution or I was a football hooligan... of course the real reason for shaving all our heads was pure sexual

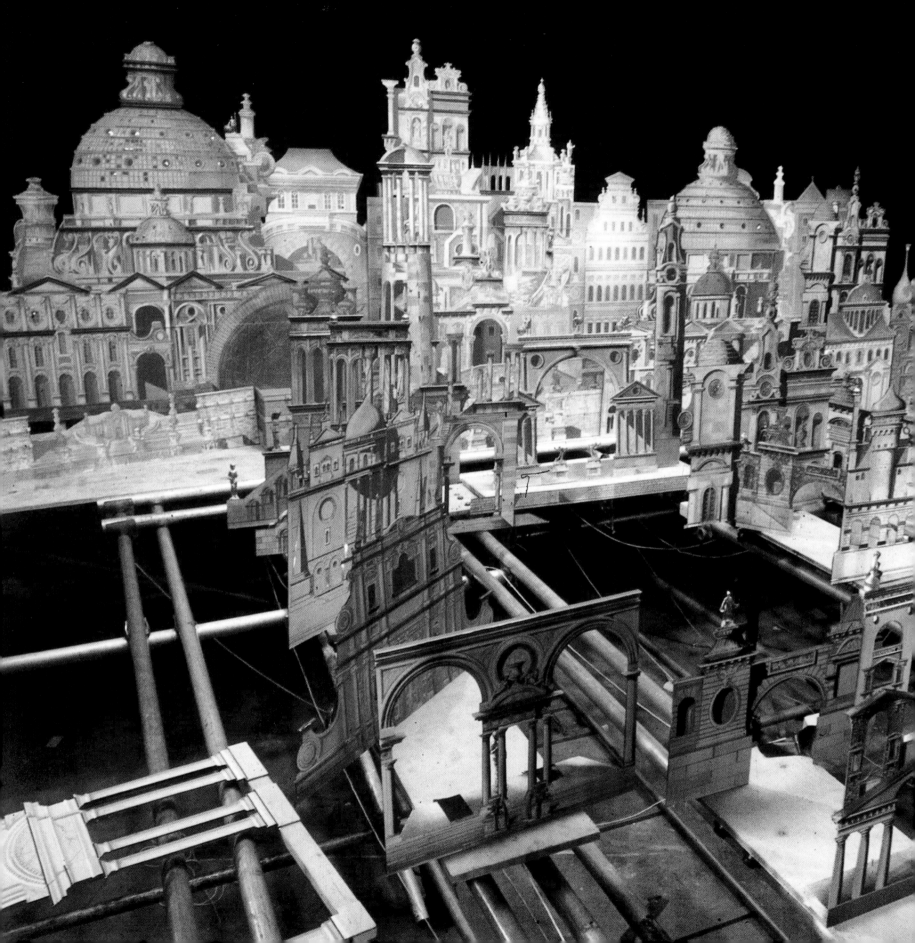

jealousy on Gilliam's part.'

Filming was then scheduled to begin on 14 September, but the costumes still weren't ready. On 12 September, a crane and some scaffolding collapsed on the still uncompleted set, postponing filming for yet another week. The rumour was, that this had been no accident.

'Thomas was an idiot because there was a crash on the set so we had to delay things, which gave us a chance to get the costumes ready,' recalls Gilliam. 'Then a month later, Thomas was out in Hollywood saying that he knocked the thing over in order to get the insurance claim, but of course we didn't get the insurance claim. I don't know the details, but I know Thomas had that done. Such was the confusion that Jake Eberts, the executive producer, turned up on the 14th for the first day of shooting, but nobody had told him we weren't shooting that day.'

With filming now scheduled for 21 September, amazingly, things got worse. The two dogs on call as the Baron's beloved Argus fell ill. Spain, where the battle scenes were to be filmed, had been hit by an outbreak of African horse fever, meaning that the numerous horses, trained for months in Rome, could not be brought into the country. Then David Puttnam was sacked from Columbia, with his successors apparently keen to distance themselves from anything they perceived to be associated with him. Without having shot a single frame, *Munchausen* was already $2 million over budget.

When filming finally began, it took place on Dante Ferretti's theatre set which had been constructed on Cinecitta's roofless stage. The first week of filming consisted of arduous night shoots, by the end of which, Gilliam and Schuhly had ceased talking to each other.

Set in a town under siege, *The Adventures of Baron Munchausen* became a film under siege, its numerous troubles as absurd and fanciful as anything the Baron himself could have concocted. The problem of unfinished costumes and sets continued throughout the first few weeks of production, compounded by that of faulty equipment when the company transferred to Almeria in Spain for more location work. The weather didn't help either.

'There was a gale where all the ships we put out in the water were destroyed and had to be rebuilt,' recounts Gilliam. 'The only costumes we had to work with when we arrived in Spain were 400 Turkish army costumes for the battle that was supposed to take place three weeks later in Zaragoza, where the set was. We only had a fifteen-foot stretch of city wall built up on a hillside, but we did the battle anyway. We planned it the night before and went in with four hundred extras, elephants, cannons, horses and everything, and shot it in a day. It couldn't have been any worse. There were the Film Finance people (the film's bonding company), strutting around in Bermuda shorts, saying, "The problem with the film is there's too many documentary crews here." At the same time we got the photo contact sheets, and in the middle of all the daily shots were pictures of Thomas back in Cinecitta in Rome, posing in his boxer shorts. These shots were taken for what he hoped would be a spread in *Playboy* magazine. It was fucking madness.'

Schuhly hadn't helped matters by touting the movie as the biggest European production since *Cleopatra*, according to Gilliam. 'All the Italians can remember is that film kept them going for years, so everything was twice the price. We built the cannons, we shipped them to Spain for, say, $12,000 and shipped them back with a Spanish company for $5,000. That's what was

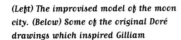

(Left) The improvised model of the moon city. (Below) Some of the original Doré drawings which inspired Gilliam

happening. The mismanagement and disorganisation was just extraordinary.'

Six weeks into principal photography, Gilliam realised the full extent of the trouble his dream project was in.

'When you make a film you have a draw-down schedule from the bank, so on week one you take out X amount of money, and it's all supposed to be controlled. I don't know how it was possible on a twenty one week shoot, but by the sixth week, all the money was gone. We were standing there with the balloon about to go up, all these extras and this really complicated shot, and there, suddenly, in the middle of the shot, is Thomas with his back to the set with a TV crew doing an interview and we were just the background for him. I thought I was tired after *Brazil*, but after *Munchausen* I thought, "Fuck, I can't stand making movies".'

With Schuhly a ghostly presence at best on set, Gilliam found himself faced not only with the insurmountable odds of bringing the Baron's lavish visuals to life using an international crew that could not communicate with each other, but also dealing with the money men, who were getting increasingly worried about the amount by which the film was going to over-run its budget. On top of that, accountants then discovered $5 million of unpaid, undeclared production bills stuffed into a desk drawer in Schuhly's office.

On 7 November, the crew returned from Spain to find the production had been closed down by the bonding company. 'When we were given our notice,' recalled actor Winston Dennis, 'I said, "That's it, the Baron's dead. It's all over bar the shouting".'

'I think people who had experience of these things,' added Charles McKeown, 'thought when films closed down, they didn't start up again.'

Gilliam was feeling the same way, and on some level was almost pleased by the result. This was his way out, his means to escape the living nightmare his cherished movie had become.

'I just thought, "Fuck, let's get out of here," but for the first time Charles McKeown got really stroppy with me and said, "You can't. You dragged everyone out here. You can't walk away from

this thing." He was the one that really forced me to sit down and solve the problem. When you get into those situations, the best thing to do is completely destroy it. If it's only half-destroyed, you kill it, and that's what Charles and I did. But out of those ashes came a semi-phoenix.'

Gilliam, McKeown and veteran first assistant director David Tomblin, who was acting as *de facto* line producer on the movie, repaired to Rome to drastically cut the script in a cost-cutting attempt to salvage the movie. 'The bonding company wanted the moon sequence out,' says McKeown, 'but we thought if you did that you had half a movie. So we de-populated the moon sequence. It would have been the most Gilliamesque sequence if it had happened, but a way out seemed to be to reduce it to the King and the Queen.'

This led to Sean Connery walking away from the production, but also to one of the movie's most imaginative – and cost-friendly – visuals: the Moon City. 'Those are literally blow-ups for the plans of what we were gonna build,' explains Gilliam. 'I mounted them on plywood, coloured them in with felt-tip markers and things. It's really crude, exactly like I used to do my animation. Dante did nice little things, like putting little sequins on pins, so when they moved there were little flicks of light. Then we pulled them on cables and pushed the camera through and it's fucking great. I hate and love those moments in equal measure. I hate being forced into doing it because the moment when you're being forced is the most awful thing. It's like squeezing a really big pimple. But then when it pops, suddenly it becomes this idea that works a treat.'

Two weeks later, the *Baron* was up and running again, with the production receiving a much-needed energy boost from the arrival of Robin Williams. The star had visited the set during its first week of production while vacationing in Europe, and one night came close to playing a small background role. His friend Eric Idle called him just as Williams' movie *Good Morning, Vietnam* was hitting the number one spot at the U.S. box office.

'He'd say, "Don't be insane. Don't put your penis in a blender",' jokes Williams. '"Why would you wanna be in a Gilliam movie, Robin? To work for nothing, for long periods of time?" But I got to come in and play that strange part. [When] they sent the offer, I thought, "It'll only be a couple of weeks, why not? It'll be fun." It wasn't like, "What are you doing with your career?" I just wanted to see what it would be like to work with him. And having seen the sets and everything, I thought, "This is going to be extraordinary".'

Williams came into a recently rewritten script and improvised a comedy *tour de force* that had the dual function of keeping the backers happy (after all, he currently had the number one film at the U.S. box office and was, therefore, the most powerful man in Hollywood *that* week) and, simply, cheering up one of the most physically drained and emotionally depressed cast and crews in cinematic history.

'I came in and kind of blew the doors down, and I think we got a chance to kick the energy back up again,' Wiliams recounts. 'They were coming back after the shutdown and working with that man, Mr Schuhly. I got the impression that he wanted to speak to me and kind of kiss ass and all sorts of things. They warned me that this guy would try to pimp the hell out of it, like getting my name above the title. But it would be false billing to say it's more than a cameo at best.' Robin Williams is credited in the final film under the name 'Ray D. Tutto'.

Despite providing a much-needed boost to the production, Williams still found himself prey to filmmaking Italian-style. 'I was working with Valentina Cortese, and because my character was so outrageous I guess she thought, "What's he doing? Terry, Terry, this is not working." I remember at one point I must have been getting good laughs because she shoved a big piece of fruit in my mouth – a giant papaya. That's one way to upstage somebody.'

Williams' energy was more of a booster shot than a cure. The production dragged on, with a demoralised Gilliam drawing it to a conclusion several weeks later. Not that all the problems ended there. Heading back to the relative security of Pinewood to do the three months of model work that followed should have been a respite, but by now the film – on course for a final budget of $46.34 million, twice its original amount – was mired down in so many financial bogs (at one point Cinecitta refused to release the negative until bills were paid), that the whole aura of disaster followed the film back home.

'We were deeply involved in it because our financial position was very precarious,' recounts Kent Houston, whose Peerless Camera were (again) handling the post-production opticals. 'We'd put in a bid that we felt was quite realistic and accurate and didn't know until we were fairly well into the movie that that bid had been completely ignored and another figure put in its place which was completely inadequate.

'We took a hiding on it and we delivered the film, but I ended up in the horrible position of being seen as the bad guy by the completion bond people, mainly because of my affiliation with Terry and my reluctance to get involved with fighting their battles for them. I just wanted to get the show done to the best of my ability. It would have been nice to have got paid for it as well.'

There are many ways to view the misadventures of the making of *Baron Munchausen*. Gilliam was in some ways to blame, if blame is the right word. His

The director on location

steadfast refusal to play the Hollywood game and get himself an agent finally backfired on him. High-priced, high-powered Hollywood suits are there to insure that the 'talent' is kept away from the seven different shades of bullshit that were obviously flying thick and fast on the *Munchausen* set. With no one in his corner, the director found himself awash in the minutiae of every aspect of his movie. The difference in working methods between the key players was obviously also a factor, with both sides seemingly unwilling to bend or bow to the other. 'It was the difference between Catholic and Protestant filmmaking,' Gilliam admits, looking back. 'They wanted to do Catholic filmmaking where I was God, Peppino was the Pope, Dante would be a cardinal at best, and all this filtered down. But everything came down via the Pope, not directly. Now if you're a Protestant filmmaker, everybody can speak directly to God, and that's what I was trying to do. And it just became a battle, and then Peppino and I weren't speaking very well, because I had a translator, which he took offence at because he spoke English.'

Of course, the press must take some of the responsibility for the pressure on Gilliam as well. Following *Brazil*, every journalist in town seemed keen to chronicle either Gilliam's new battle or his falling flat on his face.

All the more surprising, then, that the finished film should be so remarkable. As the third part of Gilliam's trilogy, it is in many ways both the most personal (it was dedicated to his three children) and the most flawed. Gilliam did himself no favours with the nature of the material, an overly difficult structure that sees the thrust of the film's 'action', in the rounding up of the Baron's assistants to save the besieged town, delayed by a lengthy preamble and an even lengthier flashback (in the Sultan's palace) before things finally get going, at which point the film abruptly shifts locations and style by going to the moon. The movie's visuals are both breathtaking and busy, with densely packed frames that are too often overpowered by an equally dense soundtrack, featuring both Michael Kamen's score and Gilliam's own soundscapes. The director admits that the final ten minutes worth of trims he made at Columbia's behest robbed the film of breathing space, and it is true.

And yet, there are truly wonderful moments in *Baron Munchausen*: the sublime image of the Baron's gondola as it moves from a starlit ocean to a gently shifting sand bank on the moon; the splendour of the Baron and Uma Thurman's Venus dancing high above the ground. The film boasted a collection of excellent performances, standouts being Oliver Reed's 'It's-grim-up-north' Vulcan and Robin Williams' brilliantly inventive King of the Moon, both of which fitted seamlessly into the world(s) Gilliam created on celluloid.

Despite generally favourable reviews, the movie flopped at the box office, completing the story of the 'over-budget disaster' that the press were keen to perpetuate. (Less than a decade later, $200 million was the going figure for a budget-busting disaster.) The four Oscar nominations the movie received did nothing to bolster its reputation, but *The Adventures of Baron Munchausen*, for all its faults, remains a thing of sporadic but deeply affecting beauty. In the strictest sense of the words, it is a 'grand folly' indeed.

BOB McCABE: Weren't you looking for a potentially easier ride after *Brazil*?
TERRY GILLIAM: Foolishly, no. I think having won the battle with the studio it was like, 'I can do anything. It's Icarus time.' And I was on a kind of roll because the effects in *Brazil* had worked very nicely, they were better than in *Time Bandits*, and it was growing towards something. When I think back on it, after *Brazil* I was

knackered, and I was feeling shagged out after a long squawk, and one of the reasons we wrote it with the little girl Sally in there was my kids. Because I was feeling like the Baron, old and worn out. And it's the kids who revivify me. Writing is great, because everything is possible when you're writing and up you come again. But the reality is, I know I have to write something around ninety pages to end up at 2 hours. Anything longer than ninety pages ends up at four hours. I get into it and it expands. It's a lesson I still haven't learned.

BM: The film is unusually structured, in that you start with these players who are telling you what you are about to see. Then you cut to a flashback and you are a good thirty minutes in before you start your adventure.

TG: A lot of people complained about that, and they may be right. We take a long time getting going. Once we get going, it rockets along. I do that with a lot of the films, it seems. There's just got to be other ways of telling stories. A lot of it comes back to Don Quixote. It's an old way of telling a story in that you're telling a tale and then someone comes along and starts telling their story, and the whole forward action is stopped and you go off in another direction. Some of them actually become stories within stories within stories. I keep wanting to do it differently. Maybe it's to say you can tell stories this way. Kids and musicians and artists — which are all kids — don't have that problem. They all love

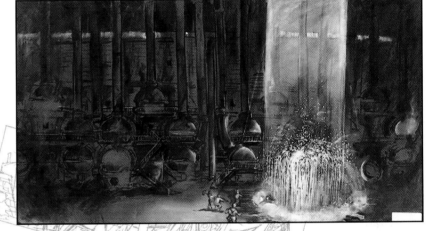

Munchausen, because they're not necessarily linear people. At one point I wanted to take out these ads of what people had said — 'Pete Townshend of The Who: "A fucking masterpiece".' I don't think narrative is the most important thing in a story. It should be, maybe.

BM: Time does play a part in all the movies, and mixing time more specifically, whether it be medieval themes in modern-day New York in *The Fisher King* or the *Time Bandits* plundering history.

TG: But I think all these times exist right now and people don't notice them. They're all there. For me it's the result of being an American living in a modern tract house built in 1950, coming to England where you've got these layers upon layers of history. A lot of the ducting in *Brazil* was a result of looking at beautiful Regency houses, Nash terrace houses, where, smashing through the cornices, is the wastepipe from the loo. It was about the loss of an aesthetic. The other thing is, they're all based on Sam Peckinpah movies like *The Wild Bunch* and *Guns in the Afternoon*. It's all about people whose time has passed and they're still there for one last hurrah, one moment of glory, and that's what *Munchausen* was very much about. It was *Guns in the Afternoon*.

BM: Jonathan Pryce is in there almost as the opposite of Sam Lowry in that he is the arch bureaucrat. And many people have read him as Sidney Sheinberg.
TG: Have they? Well that's fine. I thought he was Margaret Thatcher. And he does it with Tom Stoppard's voice. It's a very strange character.

BM: If people see Jonathan Pryce as the Sidney Sheinberg figure, then you must be Sting.

TG: I must be Sting — 'Take him out and shoot him. He sets a bad example for the others.'

BM: How much was it simple miscommunication, how much was it deliberate mismanagement and how much was it just being ripped off, left, right and centre?

TG: It was all of those things. There were problems between the English and the Italians. There were two different styles of working, but that could be handled. But there was basically no production on the thing, that was the real problem. Thomas was too busy trying to juggle all these things, keeping things going. We went through four production supervisors, four accountants and four first assistants.

BM: Was the budget based in any realistic way on what was in the script?

TG: No. I'd done the most detailed storyboards for it I'd ever done, so it was all planned. And we'd raised $23.5 million and Thomas had always said it was 30%-40% cheaper in Rome, blah, blah, blah. There's the script, there's the story-boards, there's the number of extras, and that's why the first budget came in at $60 million. It was crazed, and Thomas was in his own world. We weren't talking after the first week. There was no point in talking to him because he was just bullshitting me about everything.

BM: How much of Robin's performance was scripted, in terms of the Cartesian duel between body and mind?

TG: All of it was, but there's all sorts of ad libs in there now. But the whole shape of the thing and the basic dialogue, that wasn't there when Sean Connery was involved. We threw all of that out. Then we were left with two people on the moon and it's all about mind/body and the problems they're in. It was as simple as that. So we then wrote it all and Robin ad libbed a great deal around it. He loved being Italian; it was very funny.

BM: It's a very crammed movie both in terms of image and the sound. It's almost overpowering at times.

TG: I think it is too much. We got carried away, and it's a dangerous thing. If I were to criticise it, we were excessive on every level. The thing I never get quite right is, I seem to be unable to appreciate how complex the visuals are. To me they're normal, so I try to fill up the soundtrack to make it more rich. But I don't need to because the visuals are so dense. It's a constant fight.

BM: Do you think any element of the trouble behind the film ended up on the screen?

TG: I don't think the trouble ended up there. What is on screen is the lack of things — things we could've done better, things that might've helped the story — that we didn't get. But I don't think you see the nightmare, and, in a way, I'm proud of that. My translator assistant, who'd never worked on a film before, was constantly amazed because there was me walking round every day going 'Fuck! Shit!', and then you look at the screen and it's lovely. It wasn't a wildly over-budgeted film. It was an above-average budget for an incredibly complex film, but once the press got hold of it, it became 'Gilliam getting his comeuppance'. It was like, 'OK, he beat the studio on that last one, but now look at him — he's completely out of control.' And it really wasn't that. Simply, you get caught up in the story.

Great Unmade No. 2:
Watchmen

BY THE TIME THE FLAK FOR *Munchausen* hit, Gilliam was already talking up his next project.
Miraculously, given the financial detritus still floating around the *Baron*, Gilliam was talking of another
big budget adventure, an adaptation of the cult graphic novel *Watchmen*.

Written by Alan Moore and drawn by Dave Gibbons, *Watchmen* put a post-modern spin on the superhero comic,
analysing the damaged psyches and troubled alter-egos of a group of costumed vigilantes, made up of such
colourful figures as Rorschach, the Comedian and Dr Manhattan. Concurrent with Frank Miller's modern vision
of Batman, *The Dark Knight Returns*, it was a seminal work in a new, more adult-oriented vein of comic books.

Long-time *Brazil* fan Joel Silver, action movie maestro of such formulaic successes as *Lethal Weapon* and *Die
Hard*, had plans to turn *Watchmen* into a movie, and he wanted Gilliam to direct. 'I think the characters are great,'
says Gilliam of the aborted project. 'These tired, failed superheroes where life had gotten the better of them. And
how they've all gone in different directions, and so on. It's the idea of a world of superheroes who have all been
transformed by life.'

Batman screenwriter Sam Hamm had penned an early screenplay, which Gilliam was unsatisfied with. 'He had
made some very clever jumps, but killed it. It made it into a movie, but what did you end up with? You ended up
with these characters, but they were only shadows of the characters in an adventure. And I didn't think the book
was about that.'

Consequently, Gilliam decided to write his own screenplay, once again enlisting the help of Charles McKeown.
'We wanted to do the book as far as possible,' says McKeown. 'I think people look at a comic book and think
you're two-thirds of the way to a movie, and then you start transcribing it to the page and it's a completely
different experience. We tried to hang on to what was dramatic and what told a story about the main characters,
and cut out what we could.'

'It's really dense,' continues Gilliam, 'and when you try to reduce it down to a couple hours it's just like straight
comic book heroes again, and it doesn't have a real meaning. All the characters needed time, and I just felt we
weren't able to give them the time.'

Although work progressed on the screenplay, Joel Silver's mouth proved to be larger than his bank balance.
'Joel Silver said he had $40 million to do it, but he didn't have $40 million, he had about $24, 25 million, and we
talked about the fact that I had just made *Munchausen*, which was a huge flop that had gone over budget, and he
had just made *Die Hard 2*, which had gone way, way over and had been less successful than hoped. So the two
fools were running around Hollywood trying to raise money for this thing that's darker than anything.'

Following the poor reception of *Munchausen*, Gilliam had been eager to throw himself into a new project right
away. The collapse of *Watchmen* hit him badly. 'I was trying to avoid getting into that slump again. There's a real
tricky moment at the end of a film when, if I let it go too long before getting stuck into the next one, I just sink
into the depths of depression, and it can go on for a long time. I think after *Munchausen* the idea of jumping into
something was, "at least we can keep going." And then, of course, it didn't happen, so I did go into a spin.

Those spins seem to go on forever when I'm in them. It's the problem of not living in the future or the past,
but living in the eternity of "now". And if now is good and jolly, it's great, but if it's not, whoops! I was just dead
after *Baron Munchausen*.'

The Fisher King

THE EMOTIONAL FALLOUT FROM *Baron Munchausen* was briefly delayed by the possibility of *Watchmen*, but with that project abandoned, Terry Gilliam found himself in the depths of despair. This was compounded by the industry press unfairly turning *Munchausen* into a benchmark as the costliest flop in Hollywood's (albeit short-term) memory.

But, as Cameron Crowe so eloquently put it in *Jerry Maguire*: 'Breakdown. Breakthrough.' Gilliam's breakthrough was to finally get himself a Hollywood agent: 'I got the big boys, CAA [Creative Artists Agency]. If you're going to go with someone, go with the one with the big stick.'

CAA's response was to offer Gilliam projects he had not originated himself. One of the first of these, and in their eyes the likely contender to get the wayward filmmaker back on course, was *The Addams Family*. When the script arrived, Gilliam was disappointed to see it was little more than special effects and a lot of weak jokes, but also enclosed in the package was another script by a young writer named Richard LaGravenese.

'It must have been 1 a.m. and I was sitting in the kitchen when I started reading it. And from the first page the writing was really good and the characters were great. I knew these people, not just from the page, I knew who they were. I really identified with them. It was the perfect solution post-*Munchausen* because I didn't want to do any big stuff. I think I was going around saying I wanted to do a film about a schizophrenic, but only half his personality — that kind of crap. So this one came along — no effects, four people, a totally containable thing, and it grew into something bigger.'

Richard LaGravenese began his career as an actor who wrote monologues part-time for the other students in his acting class. He then became one half of a comedy duo, before co-writing *Rude Awakening*, the Cheech Marin–Eric Roberts' stoner-meets-yuppie vehicle. He conceived *The Fisher King* after reading Robert Johnson's psychology book *He*, which touched on

THE FISHER KING
1990 GRAIL QUEST

An early sketch

the myth of the fisher king. Immediately hooked, he set off to form this core idea into a screenplay, which went through three very distinct drafts.

'The first script was a Kafkaesque, dark, pretentious tale in which the Jeff Bridges character was a disgruntled taxi driver who meets this homeless guy on the street,' the screenwriter explains. 'And it wound up being a little like *Rain Man*, which is why I threw it out. And then I put it down for several months and picked it up again and made Jack a ne'er-do-well heir of a rubber magnate, who had to prove himself worthy of his inheritance by marrying off some sort of dim-witted cousin, which was the Lydia character. Out of that I got the Lydia character. Then I put it down again for several months before hitting upon the idea of him as a radio DJ. But the real genesis of it came out of this feeling I was having in the 1980s about the narcissism I was seeing in the culture. I found it quite disturbing and wanted to write a tale of a narcissistic man who commits a selfless act. The screen play sort of led me along that way once I made the connection between the two characters – him being a DJ and because of what he does on the air, creates a ripple effect in this other man's life, and then the responsibility he feels because of that.'

Disney soon bought the script, seemingly intent on turning it into a caper movie with James Cameron ready to fill the director's chair. 'They [Disney] wanted me to make the robbery of the Grail a set piece,' says LaGravenese, 'so they wanted me to watch movies like *Topkapi*. I did and I had to re-write my film. At the time, you have to understand, I had worked for no money for years. I'd never really earned a living, and I thought once *Fisher King* comes out everybody's going to find out I'm a fraud, so let me do what I can and get as many jobs as I can. And I just did what everybody else said at that time. I remember re-writing the robbery scene with all these laser beams and roller skates. It was ridiculous. Much to his credit, [Disney chief] Jeffrey Katzenberg said when he got that script, that the executives had led me down the wrong way, and that the second draft was not as good as the first one, but he would never make the first one because it was too dark. One person said to me at the time, "Well there are no homeless people in Jeffrey Katzenberg's world."'

The script that ended up on Terry Gilliam's kitchen table was an amalgam of drafts, although Terry would later reinstate much from LaGravense's earlier, darker versions of the tale. The film was, however, totally suitable for Gilliam. Here was a filmmaker in need of redemption presented with a tale of a man facing the same crisis. Only by committing a selfless act can Jack, the DJ figure, save Parry, the homeless product of an off-hand on-air comment that led to the loss of Parry's wife and life. Best of all, there was a Holy Grail in it, and Gilliam knew more than most filmmakers about Holy Grails. The opportunities offered by *The Fisher King* would allow Gilliam a clean slate. The filmmaker was clearly distressed at how Hollywood now viewed him. Despite having begun with the reputation of a man who could create expensive-looking movies on a shoestring, he was now labelled the excessive megalomaniac of *Munchausen*'s unfortunate press. Here was a chance to prove all that wrong, with a script that had come out of nowhere but was perfectly in tune with the filmmaker's own personal sensibilities and obsessions. The vehicle was also a chance for Gilliam to finally make a film in his home country, to take the perspective of a European exile back to New York, his former home. As for Jack and Parry, *The Fisher King* held the promise of a fresh start for Terry. Having completed one trilogy of films, Gilliam was, unknowingly, embarking on what would turn out to be another. Once again, as with *Time Bandits*, he was beginning with a project that blurred and played around with the concepts of time, from a twentieth century boy named Kevin in the court of Agamemnon to a bum named Parry on a quest for the Holy Grail in modern-day New York.

He couldn't say no, so he didn't.

For the producers Debra Hill and Linda Obst, hiring Gilliam for what was an outside-chance project anyway was a risk. 'People had seen Terry as someone whose images ruled the narrative, as opposed to characters ruling the narrative, as opposed, even, to narrative ruling the narrative,' said Obst. 'They [the studio] saw the idea of two girls and Terry Gilliam as one of the most frightening propositions they had ever encountered.'

Gilliam had one other thing going for him. Since his cameo in *Munchausen*, Robin Williams had landed two Oscar nominations (for *Good Morning, Vietnam* and *Dead Poets Society*) and had finally established himself as one of Hollywood's biggest stars. He was keen to play Parry and Terry Gilliam was on his somewhat short-list of preferred directors.

'The whole reason they came to me, I think, was to try and get Robin.' says Gilliam. 'It's a really bizarre tale because Billy Crystal had seen it first and he suggested his buddy Robin, and it was going to be him and Robin. I didn't know this at the time, but when they called me, my name had clearly come up in a meeting with Robin's managers when they were trying to get this off the ground. And they talked about which directors he wanted to work with and all the others were working, except me. So I said "yes" and my first job was to convince Robin to do it.'

'When I read *The Fisher King*,' offers Williams, 'they mentioned Terry. He was the only person to do it. It had all the hallmarks of the things he had done. The idea of Quixote in Manhattan, and there's so many gothic elements to Manhattan that he fit perfectly.'

In taking on *The Fisher King*, Terry Gilliam was breaking all his own rules. He was making a film he hadn't written; he was filming in America; he was working for a major studio – Tri-Star, ironically part of the Columbia group that had backed *Munchausen* – and he was willing to give up final cut to prove he could bring the movie in on time and budget. Also, he was forsaking an abundance of special effects to focus on a character piece, rich in emotion and providing four stand-out roles (two of which would later receive Academy Award nominations). With a characteristic feeling of not knowing exactly where he was going, but sensing he was on the right path, Gilliam jumped in head first.

Gilliam directing Robin Williams on set

Robin Williams was set as Parry (named for Parsifal, the fool or young knight in the Grail myth). The trick now was finding the right elements to balance him. Everyone from the afore-mentioned Billy Crystal to Bruce Willis to Daniel Day Lewis to Bill Murray to Kevin Kline were considered, some very briefly.

'It was only after I saw *The Fabulous Baker Boys* on a plane flying from L.A. to New York,' Gilliam recalls of his decision to cast Jeff Bridges, 'that I thought "fuck he can do it." I always thought he was great, but I just didn't think he could handle the fast, verbal shit. So I jumped off the plane and said "We've got to have Jeff." Getting a meeting with Jeff, though, was miserable. The advantage was we were both with the same agency, but it was like setting up Gorbachev and Reagan. They didn't want me to have a meeting with Jeff unless it was a firm offer, and I said it can't be a firm offer until I meet him. So then we met and he spent the whole time telling me he didn't think he was right for the part, and that someone like Jimmy Woods ought to play it. I asked him to do a reading, which he's never done before, and he didn't want to do it. But I got him and Mercedes [Ruehl, cast as Jack's lover Anne] to read, and Jeff was awful. He's just not confident enough to do it unless it's definite. So there I am,

sitting on the phone to Mercedes Ruehl, who really had no reputation or anything, saying, "What do you think, can he do it?" '

Bridges was cast and Gilliam completed his ensemble with Amanda Plummer as Lydia, the new light of Parry's life. 'We read and we worked with different people,' recalls Robin Williams of the casting process. 'I remember when he picked Amanda. She has this amazing quality of looking downright awkward and geeky, yet then the next moment looking so beatific, and that's what he wanted – that she could look so gorgeous and almost Renaissance. You look at her a certain way and she's totally hysterical and vulnerable. Same thing with Mercedes, and Jeff, God, Jeff is the best. He's so Buddhist about how he works. He looks forward to accidents and says "that's a gift, go with it." And I realised, yeah, that's it, you're right. If something is a mistake, build on that. It was really interesting. We had a wonderful combination.'

One role was cast right from the start: New York would play the world the characters found themselves in. On returning to America, Gilliam had found himself in probably the most photographed, and photogenic, city on earth. His task was to discover a new vision of it. This was partly achieved by racing Red Knights down the Upper East Side and partly by having rush-hour commuters waltz in Grand Central Station. Three other things helped: location, location, location. Gilliam set about defining his film by the places he filmed. LaGravenese's script had Jack living in a downtown loft. Gilliam placed him at the top of a razor-edged glass high-rise next to Carnegie Hall. Ironically, when Gilliam suggested that Jack should live in this desperately modern amalgam of glass, steel and power, he did not realise that the apartment he was pointing to from the street below actually belonged to Mike Ovitz, head of Gilliam's own agency, CAA. 'But you choose something,' he explains. 'It's a knife-edge building and that tells you something. And Parry, in the script, didn't live like I had it. The first homeless bit is by the Manhattan bridge, and it is a very specific place – a real place with real homeless people living there, who unfortunately got in a fight amongst themselves and burnt down their shanty town just before we started filming there. We had to give them materials to build a new shanty town – but it was under that bridge, and it's like you're at the foundation of a civilization almost.'

New York, of course, had played host to Gilliam back in the mid-1960s when he worked on *Help!* magazine. 'I think it was the same, except I was using it rather than it was using me,' he says of returning. 'Living in New York sets the tempo, and we were able to control the tempo, but only a bit. Shooting in New York is outrageous because the world does not stop for you.'

Robin Williams also held memories of the city. He studied at the prestigious Julliard School and busked a living as a street mime before finding success in stand-up and the sitcom *Mork and Mindy*. 'I had gone to school there and had wonderful experiences. It's wonderful because part of *The Fisher King* is the romance, and my memories of New York are of being madly in love during the spring there, when it is the most romantic city in the world. My other, negative, memory of it is being there and almost having a nervous breakdown when I was going to school. I was totally alone and isolated in the winter, and that's when it's at its worst.'

The Fisher King was scheduled to shoot for twelve weeks, six on location and six shooting interiors in L.A. Eager to prove himself – or rather prove himself *again* – to the filmmaking community, Gilliam, driven as always by a perverse nature, began his first day of filming by deciding to make a Spaghetti Western. 'I had this weird idea that I was going to shoot the whole thing like a Sergio Leone Western, and there's only a couple of shots left that relate to that. One of them was our first day's shooting, when Jack finds Parry sitting on top of a car as Jack walks across the street. Well it's a shot that's actually a Western shot, because there's the car and the legs walk into the foreground. And the gun hand is there. It was a total Leone shot. You grab a silly idea like that and it gives you a focus, at least to begin with.'

Gilliam got on with the filming in hitherto unknown style – no shutdowns, no massive script rewrites, no improvised monsters, no catatonic retreats to bed. The only troublesome moment came when a woman threw a bucket of water out of her apartment window at the Red Knight.

(Above) Gilliam's original, unused poster art, complete with DaVinci cut-out, 1991. (This page and right) Gilliam's storyboards

'We were shooting one time on Columbus Avenue and it was like ten o'clock at night,' laughs Robin Williams, 'and this woman who was angry threw a bucket of water out. It just barely missed the stuntman on the horse. So these two New York cops go upstairs and knock on the woman's door and the cops said "Ma'am, if you do that again, I'm throwing *you* out the window. Have a nice night." '

The shooting went so smoothly that when the New York weather threw Gilliam a lemon, hey, he made lemonade. Or Chinese food, as the case may be. 'The only interior we did in New York, apart from Grand Central Station, which is more like an exterior, was the Chinese restaurant,' Gilliam recalls. 'This is craziness. We were in New York for five weeks shooting with no weather cover, and we got caught out one night in the park, and we couldn't shoot because it was raining and the only thing we could do was head down to the Chinese restaurant for the interior. We had to get down there that night and literally build the set and then shoot it. And it was the only scene we'd done that we hadn't rehearsed. There were certain lines we had to get, but the rest is ad-libbed, and I just did take after take after take and I didn't know how I was going to cut it. I had no coverage. So what I worked out later were those wipes, and they worked brilliantly. And the shot I was really pleased with was the end shot when Robin was singing "Lydia the Tattooed Lady" and we pull back over the tabletops. But we didn't have a crane arm there to do this shot, so the guys built one out of two-by-four pieces of wood. It's really old-fashioned filmmaking – as the camera's pulling back, the prop guys are sliding the tables into place. There's one part where you see a lantern swing in the foreground, which was the only bit that got bumped. It was an interesting evening because we were all as tired as shit, and that's where Robin comes into his own. It must've been about three or four in the morning when everybody's really flagging, he did a twenty minute stand-up routine. He could see the crew was tired and he just started doing it, and he sort of incorporated everybody in the crew into the routine. He had something to say about everybody and it was great.'

Williams remembers another moment that saw him working at his peak on-camera, as he demonstrated the benefits of a good bowel movement for Jeff Bridges' character. 'One time I did a rehearsal and I could never get back to it. I think it made Terry laugh so hard he fell off a chair. Somehow in the process, I should say I almost shat myself, but I got to the point where I was pushing so hard I did actually start to see stars. At the moment I let go, there they were, and it was a real explosive thing and Terry just went berserk.'

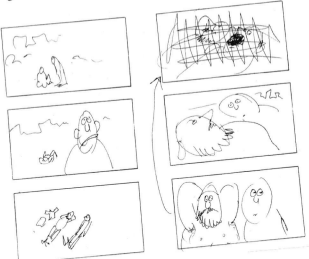

The most visually splendid moment of the film was unscripted and came about during Terry Gilliam's location scout of Grand Central Station. Gilliam stood looking down on the concourse, watching the flow of rush-hour commuters, then turned and said to those in earshot, 'Wouldn't it be great if they all looked over at the person next to them and fell in love and started waltzing?'

'That scene is a wonderful example of how he expanded the script and made it better,' says LaGravenese. 'In the original script I had Jack sitting with Parry and he hears this homeless woman singing – there is a real woman in Grand Central Station who does that – and a crowd of people begin to gather and he becomes a part of them. He looks in the crowd and sees businessmen, secretaries, mothers and all these different types of people, and for a moment he feels a part of a community. Then I realised that having Jack feel a part of a community at that point was too early for the character, so focussing on Parry and allowing the audience to get inside his world was absolutely the right idea, and it elevated it without dialogue and with this wonderful imagery.'

Gilliam had to be talked into his impulse of going with the waltz. 'It took about a month for them to convince me

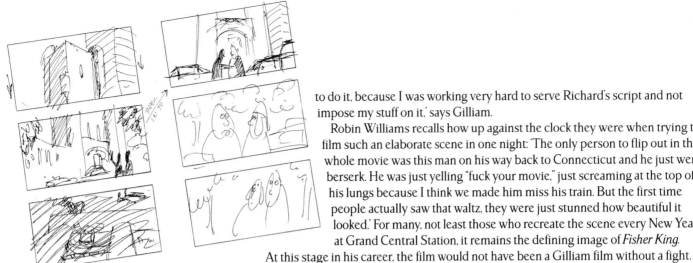

to do it, because I was working very hard to serve Richard's script and not impose my stuff on it,' says Gilliam.

Robin Williams recalls how up against the clock they were when trying to film such an elaborate scene in one night: 'The only person to flip out in the whole movie was this man on his way back to Connecticut and he just went berserk. He was just yelling "fuck your movie," just screaming at the top of his lungs because I think we made him miss his train. But the first time people actually saw that waltz, they were just stunned how beautiful it looked.' For many, not least those who recreate the scene every New Year's at Grand Central Station, it remains the defining image of *Fisher King*.

At this stage in his career, the film would not have been a Gilliam film without a fight. Thankfully, this time around, it proved to be no more than a mild fracas, despite the film company having changed hands once again during production, when Columbia was bought out by Sony. New studio head Mike Medavoy wanted Gilliam to cut his 137 minute movie down to a more manageable two hours.

'From the very first screening, the numbers were great,' says Gilliam. 'But if they're good or bad, they can always be better as far as the studios are concerned. They wanted it down to two hours. We had a meeting the next day after another screening and we cut out some bits and we only lost four minutes. The next day I'm on my way to the airport and I get a call from an executive saying the numbers are the same, but it played so much better. And I said "I don't care if it played better, the cards are the same. I'm not making the cuts." And I got on a plane and left. Then I got a letter from Mike Medavoy the next week, and it was ridiculous because it was clearly meant for his superiors in Japan, and it was saying that I hadn't co-operated and I hadn't played the game, that they had given us everything and I hadn't repaid the favour. It was a real ass-covering thing, and it pissed me off. So I wrote a letter back to him denying all this nonsense and saying this is crap, you've got a good movie and you should be behind it.'

The Fisher King changed Terry Gilliam's world and the world view of Terry Gilliam. Here was a mythical land known to be New York City. Here was a quest steeped in legend and fantasy that found its fulfilment in reality, an escape from madness, a world Sam Lowry might have found if he had come out the other side. Parry took that journey with a great deal of help from Jack. Perhaps most significantly, here was a film

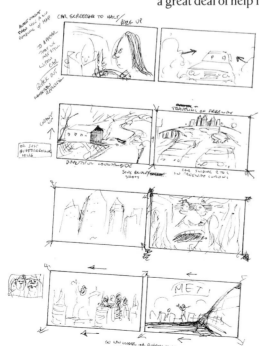

from a special effects-heavy fantasist that not only spent four weeks on top of the U.S. box office but landed two of its principal cast members — Williams and Ruehl — a shot at an Academy Award. The fact that Bridges was overlooked for a nomination remains one of the Academy's many potentially punishable offences over the years.

More than anything, *The Fisher King* was the movie that melded Gilliam's inner visions to the outside world – the movie through which Gilliam found he wasn't alone, that other people's ideas could find room to run rampant through his brain and be brilliantly diffused through his lens. The film showed both him and every potential employer that he could not just deliver on time, but deliver the goods. It was, in short, a remarkable film and his best movie to date.

This period should have been the beginning of a glorious stage for Terry Gilliam. He had just turned fifty years old, he was riding high in the box office

charts, Hollywood was his for the asking, and he fell for it. 'I got caught in the worse possible thing. Being fifty, I thought I would know better. I let the barrier fall down and suddenly all these really interesting things were there, and I was running from this one to that one. I thought I was old enough to deal with it, but I wasn't. I became fragmented, and I wasted a lot of time, basically.'

It would be five years before Terry Gilliam made another film.

BOB McCABE: It must have been strange, sitting in your kitchen, reading that script for the first time. Great characters, great dialogue, and then suddenly there's a Holy Grail in there.

TERRY GILLIAM: I think their impression of me was 'he does Holy Grail movies.' I approached it like a fairy tale. I was very specific in my thinking — because it was contemporary didn't matter. We had the Grail. We had a knight roaming around, a madman who's perceiving the world in this twisted way. The Fisher King's kingdom is New York, which is a dead

place, surrounded by an ocean — a moat. It's isolated. Within that there are castles of different sorts. Jack lives in the modern castle, a totally barren place — it's steel and glass. There's a video shop at the bottom of a brick building, which is like the peasant's hut in the forest, with these great tree trunks, or skyscrapers, growing up. Then you've got Lydia, who's sort of a princess in a great stone castle, a prisoner in this office building.

And with Parry we start going into death and transfiguration, which is part of the verticality of it. It's a very vertical movie. Jack plummets from the heights, not just to the earth, which he does, but he has to die effectively. That's why, when he's attacked by the kids, it's a kind of death, and he ends up in a grave, a cave under the ground, and he has to rise up again. So I was playing with all that mythological imagery in my head. We made Parry's place this thing in the bowels of the earth with a Wagnerian furnace and everything. The weird thing about the film is usually there's this central character that is me, but on this one I was totally schizophrenic. Having said I was going to make a film about a schizophrenic, it turned out it was me. And I was torn between which point of view to choose, whether it was Jack's or Parry's. I had to reshoot part of the scene where Parry rescues Jack at the beginning because I was shooting it from the wrong point of view. Whatever happens at that point, it has to be Jack's point of view; it can't be Parry's. I eventually settled down and got that one right.

BM: You'd hit fifty at this time. Do you think it influenced the movie?

TG: I'm sure it did, and I'd been slightly chastened after my excesses with *Munchausen* and *Brazil*. All of those were battles and I was tired. I didn't want to keep hammering at doors and banging my head against the wall. But it was inherent in the script, too. There was a real character warmth in the thing. My concern when we were making it was to avoid sentimentality. I was scared to death of it becoming soppy, and I think we did avoid it.

BM: It's very definitely a post-yuppie movie.

TG: The 1980s were all about the 'me' generation, and the film is the opposite of that. You've got an egocentric character at the beginning who has to give, who has to serve something other than himself, something greater. It's about re-discovering love, humanity, relationships, all those things. He's got to go out and perform selfless acts, and in a strange way that's what I was doing on the film. I wanted to do a selfless act. It wasn't my script. I was serving the film, I was serving Richard's idea, and I went at it very specifically in that frame of mind. I felt that after *Munchausen* I had to reclaim something by not doing my stuff. So the Jeff character is about learning to be selfless. All through the film we emphasise those moments more, like when Jeff gives Robin money when he goes back to him, realising who he is. That wasn't in the script. That was an 1980s thing, thinking money will buy everything. It's an anti-1980s film.

BM: Again, if anything, there are almost too many elements in there, from homelessness to the shadow of AIDS. And halfway through you stop the Grail story and have a romantic comedy for a while, then you go back to the plot.

TG: That's one of the reasons I liked the script, because it was like that. Each thing has its moment. And you can

criticise it for that, but I liked that. I like the fact that it's never straight down the line. And I think the twists and turns in it were what kept me interested in the whole thing. I remember I was at Sundance doing a workshop with Quentin Tarantino [on the script for *Reservoir Dogs*], and when we showed it there, Stanley Donen was present. He had an evening where he showed clips from all his musicals. And I said afterwards that had I seen all those clips before I'd done *Fisher King*, I would've dedicated the film to him and thanked him. Because the film is very like a musical, and I didn't realise how much Stanley Donen had influenced me over the years. It was kind of like when I read *Reservoir Dogs*. It was all over the place, but it didn't matter because the thrust of the thing was so good. And it was the same with Richard's screenplay. It's like the scene in Grand Central Station with Tom Waits. The studio wanted that out because it wasn't advancing the narrative. But it works really well. What studios don't realise is if you pull that out, then the waltz isn't as good because you need to be taken down into some kind of reality before you spring off into some kind of wonderful fantasy.

BM: You could have found a safer movie to convince Hollywood you could play by their rules.
TG: It seemed like a very safe movie to me. I read it and I thought 'This is easy. It's just a real romp this one.' I think what I did is, I emphasised all those moments and made more out of them, more than another director might have done. For me, it was an interesting thing to see what I do because this was the first film where I felt like a film director. On all the other ones I felt like a filmmaker. It was the first film I directed, let's put it that way.

BM: *Pinocchio*, one of your key influences, makes an appearance, in wooden puppet form.
TG: I added that. It was what the Jack character is about — to become a real boy. And that's what he becomes in the film, a real human being. And I can't remember when I got Pinocchio, but it was such a good character to have with Robin holding him.

BM: Logistically, how easy was it to stage a waltz in Grand Central Station?
TG: We had one night to do it. We got control of the station at 11pm and we had it until 6.10 in the morning. All these extras were supposed to be waltzers, and we very quickly learned they weren't. We had eight choreographers out there teaching people, but we didn't get shooting until two or three in the morning because we were running a dance school for three or four hours at Grand Central Station. The sound system was supposed to be playing back a waltz, and the sound in Grand Central Station is so echoey you couldn't hear it. So it ended up with the main choreographer with a bullhorn on a ladder, going, '1,2,3... 1,2,3... ' We shot the waltz in two hours, using five cameras. It was just mad. The top shot was the hardest one because it gives away everything. We had a thousand people, and we looked down and it wasn't full, so in the final film I had to double-print it. I took two shots and superimposed them and doubled the number of people. If you look closely you can see a number of ghost people there, going through each other. It was the only way to fill it up.

(L-r) Jeff Bridges, Terry Gilliam, Robin Williams, Mercedes Ruehl

BM: There's a lovely image in the movie when Parry says goodnight to Lydia and catches his split image in the glass panel of the door.
TG: That came out of location scouting. We found a couple of places we were interested in, and I was inside and looked out the front door and a bevelled edge did that thing. And then, of course, the location we used didn't have that bevelled edge door, so we had to make a piece of

bevelled glass and stick it in there. By going out and finding locations and finding things, you stumble across other things. It's all about that. It's the 'tripping over something' approach to filmmaking, is all it is. It works a treat.

BM: Having given up your right to final cut, presumably Tri-Star could have cut the film down to two hours if they had wanted to.

TG: It was partly that they knew there was a good film there, and they didn't want to alienate me. It's that thing of the longer you're there and the more they know you, the less likely they are to try and take something away. I also realised these people were non-confrontational. We were lucky to get non-confrontational types. They're basically fearful people, and if they think you're good and if they think you've made a good film, they don't want to chance alienating you. Here's how silly it gets: when it came to doing post-sync, we needed Robin in England to do it, and in Robin's contract he's got to fly with his wife, so he had two first class tickets. They had a baby at this time which, of course, needed a nanny. So suddenly we're talking about four first class tickets, which is a great deal of money, and the studio was asking if I couldn't go to L.A. and do it because then it would just be one. And I said no because we're trying to finish the film. I don't have the time. It's the only practical way of working. Me going back and forth on planes kills me. We've got too much work to do, Robin should be there. So all you've got to say is 'no'. Robin's been paid $6 million plus, surely he can afford to bring his kid and nanny. But they [Tri-Star] wouldn't [approach Williams]. They were going to pay for the whole thing because nobody was going to go to Robin, or go to his agents, and say 'no you can't,' because they didn't want to alienate him.

A Terry Gilliam sketch of the Red Knight. (Right) The real thing

BM: You have said that it was the first film you were truly satisfied with. Is it?
TG: I think so, because I don't think I had nearly the anxiety and the nightmare uncertainty of it. It was what it was: clear. It was well-received, too; nobody walked out. It felt like 'I know what this film is,' which was great. And maybe the trick was — it wasn't mine. Richard made a really good film. So much of it is tricking my own fucking brain. That's what's so terrifying about it.

BM: It was also the first film you made with nary a Python in sight.
TG: I finally grew up. I became a real boy.

Great Unmade No.3:
'It was the best of times, it was the worst of times'

TERRY GILLIAM FOUND HIMSELF WITH A NUMBER ONE MOVIE on his hands and all of Hollywood lined up, eager to offer plaudits. *The Fisher King* had broken all the rules Gilliam had set for himself, and now he broke another – he bought into all that Hollywood had to offer. He could make the movies he always wanted to make. 'I was like the kid in the candy store: "I want that one, oh no, shit, I want that one." Having gone to Hollywood, played the game, won the game, and then said "Now I want to do this," I thought I understood the rules.' His next projects proved otherwise.

A Scanner Darkly (1991)
Partly inspired by his reaction to *Blade Runner*, and the feeling that science fiction writer Philip K. Dick's material had never been successfully transferred to the screen, Gilliam enlisted his *Fisher King* collaborator Richard LaGravenese and opted for Dick's novel, *A Scanner Darkly*.

'Wanting to do it was probably a reaction to *Total Recall* because I'm fed up with Philip K. Dick's books not being made. *The Truman Show* is Philip K. Dick – everyone steals from Dick and they never credit him. I was asked to direct *The Truman Show* and I didn't because I thought it was sub-Philip K. Dick. That writer has greater depth in him than anybody has dealt with.'

Gilliam's enthusiasm was riding high on *Scanner*. The team that had just delivered Tri-Star one of its biggest hits of the year in *The Fisher King* went to the studio to seek financing for their new project. But Tri-Star would not even give them development money. Where before Gilliam would have stuck with his project and shopped it around, even funding the scripting process himself, the allure of the Hollywood stash proved too much. *A Scanner Darkly* was abandoned in favour of the next project.

A Connecticut Yankee in King Arthur's Court (1991)
Karate Kid scribe Robert Mark Kamen had been working on an adaptation of Mark Twain's satirical classic, *A Connecticut Yankee in King Arthur's Court*. The story had surfaced on the screen in many forms before, with everyone from Bing Crosby to Bugs Bunny in the lead, but no one had ever attempted to tell the tale the way Twain intended, as a cautionary comment on warfare and America's unerring sense of intervention. Producer Jerry Weintraub thought Gilliam had the right edge for the project.

'I hated Robert's script. When he asked why, I said, "Because I read the book again and the script is bullshit. It's nothing to do with the book." The book is dark. It's got real weight to it because it's about American meddling – Yankee know-how, going out there and doing what the Yankee thinks is best for that particular society, and fucking it up totally. That was something I've always felt strongly about. Robert kept saying "they won't accept a script like that." So we sat down and worked on the thing and they liked it. King Arthur's court intrigued me because I wanted to do a dark period piece again. We got the script pretty close. I got Robert writing in a way he hadn't written in years. He was on a contract for, like, a million dollars a year just to work as a script doctor, and he'd become so corrupted by the system and so self-censoring that he wouldn't even write things.'

Gilliam spent several months in 1991-92 working on the screenplay, but although there was studio interest in the project, he became swayed by a shot at another literary classic.

A Tale of Two Cities (1993)
Mel Gibson had made his name as a post-apocalyptic law-bringer in the *Mad Max* movies, and then again as an on-the-edge, and sometimes over it, cop in Joel Silver's *Lethal Weapon* series. By 1993, he had turned his hand to directing, with *The Man Without a Face*, and was looking for a potentially more Academy-friendly project. He settled upon Charles Dickens' *A Tale of Two Cities*. British screenwriter Don McPherson had written the screenplay.

'I really liked it. I thought it made Dickens and David Lean come together somehow. It told the tale well. They had been developing it for a couple of years for Mel and so I went out and met him, and we got on very nicely. But Mel was uncertain about whether he really wanted to do it or not, because there was something he was more interested in, which he asked if I might want to direct, a medieval film about a Scotsman, William Wallace. I said, "no thanks, I don't want to do it. I've done medieval films".'

Gibson eventually abandoned *A Tale of Two Cities*, then budgeted at $60 million, to make his William Wallace movie, *Braveheart*, which went on to win several Oscars, including a Best Director statuette for Gibson. Gilliam struggled to find a replacement, with both Harrison Ford and Daniel Day Lewis showing some interest. Ultimately, Liam Neeson signed on as lead.

The Hollywood Years

This reduced the budget to what should have been a manageable $31 million, but Warner Bros, who were backing the project, were only prepared to go up to $26 million with Neeson on board, despite his recent Academy Award nomination for Spielberg's *Schindler's List*. The project collapsed.

Looney Tunes (1994)

By this time, Gilliam's creative juices were being stoked by a story of a man who turns into a cartoon. Robert Gordon had written a script named *Loony Tunes* that embraced the recent advances made in computer-generated effects, allowing the star of the film to move and act with all the unlimited parameters of a cartoon figure.

'We were spending a lot of time reworking the script,' Gilliam recalls. 'I wasn't writing it, but we would sit down and have long sessions and say "this story should go here, here's a good gag." It's that kind of stuff. It's co-writing, but it's not actually writing the stuff. I think he wrote it because he's a lover of Tex Avery. It's wonderful stuff. Where *The Mask* [the similarly themed Jim Carrey vehicle made that same year] is a guy who just does it, zap, this is a guy who is really cool. He's a bit of an asshole, but he's cool. Then suddenly he starts turning into this cartoon, so when he sees a girl his jaw drops and his tongue rolls across the floor, and it's awful for him because this is not what he wants to be like.' Again, the project didn't materialise.

Quasimodo (1994)

In 1994, Gilliam was presented with an adaptation of Victor Hugo's *The Hunchback of Notre Dame*. At the time the project was set up at Disney, who were also in the process of readying their animated musical version of the same tale.

'We were looking for locations and Gerard Depardieu was going to play the lead. The script was O.K. It was a very weird feeling, something wasn't right here. It was a combination of people working on the project. And when I saw the trailer for the animated version, I thought, "Oh shit, those are the shots I was gonna do." They're really exhilarating shots round the cathedral. The animated version has got some really good camera moves in it and some really good detail. I liked the idea of doing a medieval melodrama, and the good thing about the script was it stayed true the book – people died at the end. No one's really done the book properly. The best thing about working on it was getting to roam around every inch of Notre Dame. That was great. That was worth the whole price of admission.'

Tesla (1994)

Around this time Gilliam toyed with the idea of a movie based on the life of Nikola Tesla, the inventor of alternating current. 'Our entire civilisation depends on Nikola Tesla and he's forgotten,' Gilliam opines. 'He was this electrical genius. You think Marconi invented the radio. No, the New York Supreme Court posthumously agreed, Tesla invented the radio. He was one of the richest people in New York. He was on the cover of *Time* magazine and nobody knows about him, and he fascinates me, as he's fascinated a lot of people. Orson Welles wanted to do something on him. He was best friends with Mark Twain. Debussey used to come over to his place and play the piano. All that lab stuff in James Whale's *Frankenstein*, that's all Tesla stuff. He literally did bring down lightning from the clouds. He invented a machine that created an earthquake in New York – little things like that...

'So this whole thing is extraordinary. I don't know how to make a movie out of it, but I keep thinking about it. There were a couple of scripts going around. David Lynch had done one. There was a really good book out on him which I gave to Tom Stoppard, hoping he would get interested, but he passed on it.'

By this time, Gilliam had not made a movie for over three years. 'I think they all had possibilities. I don't think I regret them, I just think you spend a lot of time and you get pretty pissed off. And I think I was incredibly stupid to let myself get sucked into Hollywood. The only thing it taught me is to be a bit more sympathetic to producers, who are spending a ridiculous amount of time trying to get things done and they make $25,000 on a film in development. Some of these people spend years and years on something, and that's why they end up having to have so many projects on the go at one time. I don't know how many $25,000s you need to survive in Hollywood, but you need quite a few. Producers in Hollywood are masochists basically, most of them. If they're not, then they're sadists. There's nothing in between. There are the ones that make it and then become brutal. Then there are the others who are really much more intelligent, sensitive people who end up being kind of masochists, like battered wives.'

'THE HUMAN RACE WAS DOOMED... Its only hope for survival was time... emissaries in time to summon the past and the future to the aid of the present. One man was chosen for his obsession with images from the past, but he is never sure whether he invents or dreams.'

This excerpt sounds like the pitch screenwriters David and Janet Peoples made to sell their time-spanning odyssey *Twelve Monkeys*, but it is, in fact, the opening narration from *La Jetee*, Chris Marker's remarkable 1962 short. *La Jetee* blended still photography with a haunting, existential debate on Armageddon. It was the inspiration for the Peoples' screenplay, which would become the second movie where Terry Gilliam worked on material generated by someone else. That the Peoples should interest Gilliam was unsurprising. David had scripted *Unforgiven*, one of Gilliam's favourite Hollywood movies of the 1990s, and had also penned the screenplay for *Blade Runner*, the movie that both inspired and confounded the filmmaker. There was, of course, another incentive to working with the script. 'This one actually had the money,' Gilliam quipped at the time. 'We reached the point where all the other projects kept collapsing for various reasons. This one wouldn't go away... So I said, "It's time to go to work".'

Producer Charles Roven was greatly impressed with how the Peoples had taken the core essence of *La Jetee* and developed it into *Twelve Monkeys*. 'The Peoples wrote a script that, because of its time travel aspect and its different worlds aspect, needed a director who could give it a fantastic visual sense,' he says, 'and the perfect director for it was Terry Gilliam.'

Gilliam needed to make a film and, much like Richard LaGravenese's *Fisher King*, *Twelve Monkeys* offered him an array of long-time personal obsessions with which to play. All of his movies had experimented with time, whether it was outmoded storytellers like the Baron, trying in vain to die in the Age of Reason, or bandit dwarves whose view of history was limited strictly to the potential booty available, or the mixed retro-future design of *Brazil*, or the classical quest on Fifth Avenue of *The Fisher King*. The theme of madness was also prominent here, in all its myriad forms, from the maniacal tics of Jeffrey Goines to the deep-rooted psychosis of Cole. Once again, Gilliam had found himself presented with material that cried out for him to realise it, but unlike before, he was not that quick to jump.

'The whole thing was getting very frustrating,' Gilliam admits. 'The joke was to have been so smart and avoiding Hollywood for all those years, then at fifty thinking I'd got it sussed, but then blowing it. When the script arrived I didn't leap at it immediately, but it was a very intriguing script and nothing like that had come along. Chuck [Roven] was the one who created the momentum. I'd seen *Unforgiven* and it geed me up because I thought David's writing on that was amazing, and we all met and we all liked each other.'

One of the things that persuaded Gilliam was the glorious irony involved. *Twelve Monkeys*, a project for which he was being actively sought, was to be made by Universal Pictures, his *Brazil*-time adversaries.

Gilliam's initial wariness of the project stemmed from the fact that he was clearly lowering his head into the lion's mouth that was Hollywood, causing a feeling of unease that was exacerbated when the studio insisted the film — budgeted at a modest $30 million — be made star-heavy. 'Their concern, which seems to be the main concern in Hollywood these days, is the opening week-end, and to guarantee the opening weekend they want stars,' explains Gilliam. 'So at that point I really wanted Jeff Bridges or

Nick Nolte to play the lead, but the studio wouldn't go along with it. They wanted a bigger star and they started throwing all sorts of names at me – all the Toms. I said "No, these guys are all wrong," and I actually walked away. Then I got a call saying Bruce Willis was interested. We'd spent an afternoon together during *The Fisher King*, because at one point he was very keen for the part that Jeff Bridges did, and I really liked him. So we went to New York and met. And that's the right situation to deal with Bruce Willis or any of those guys, because they've got to come to you wanting desperately to do it. Then you know they are in the right frame of mind, and you can discuss terms.'

Like Gilliam's previous top-liner, Robin Williams, Bruce Willis had made one of the most impressive TV debuts in recent memory – as the wisecracking private eye David Addison on *Moonlighting* – before moving to the big screen in a series of, at best, average vehicles. While Williams finally found movie fame by bringing his hugely inventive stand-up to *Good Morning, Vietnam*, Willis broke the curse of *Blind Date* and *Sunset* by dropping the jokes and stripping down to vest and a .45 in the *Die Hard* series. His status as action man had made him one of the biggest stars in town, but Willis had always struggled to show that he could do more, by taking smaller, less seen and less showy roles in movies like *Billy Bathgate* and *Nobody's Fool*. This side of his career came to a head in Quentin Tarantino's *Pulp Fiction*, in which Tarantino not only resurrected John Travolta's career, but showed the world that Bruce Willis was a more multidimensional actor. Now Willis wanted to play the lead role of the time-travelling Cole, and this was the man Gilliam wanted to work with.

'We had a long talk about this film and what I wanted and what I didn't want from him, and we agreed,' says Gilliam. 'Part of the excitement for me was the chance to transform Bruce, to show another side of him. That's what he wanted desperately. It's very hard not to want to help somebody change the world's perception of them. If there's anything I'm trying to do, it's change perceptions. We all have different work habits and no matter how hard he tries not to be a star, with all of the surroundings, he's been with it too long, and his terms of coming naked to the project are not where I'm coming from. So we met in the middle somewhere.' Translated, this means Willis brought along his personal driver, bodyguard and mobile gym, but left the usual dozen-plus 'entourage' at home.

During the filming of *Twelve Monkeys*, Brad Pitt was named 'the sexiest man alive' by the, let's be honest, not very influential *People* magazine. When Pitt first met Gilliam, he was known mainly as the scene-stealing rogue of *Thelma and Louise*, the walking quiff of *Johnny Suede* and the Robert Redford alter-ego of *A River Runs Through It*. Pitt was also a big fan of Terry Gilliam and eager to work with him, even if the filmmaker did not believe he was up to the task.

'He wanted to escape from the blonde bimbo thing,' Gilliam says. 'Immediately after I said yes, I regretted it. I put him together with Stephen Bridgewater, this ex-DJ who had worked with Jeff on *Fisher King*, and after the first day, Stephen calls me and says, "What have I ever done to you to deserve this? He can't do it. The guy's got no breath control, he's got a lazy tongue. It's terrible." Then the weeks went by and eventually he said, "Yeah, he can do it." Brad was supposed to be sending me tapes all the time of his progress, which he was not doing, and that was making me crazy and convinced that I'd fucked up. It was only through Stephen that I could keep track of how it was going. It was really hard work for Brad to get himself where he got to. By the end of his first day he was like a limp rag. He'd expended so much energy that he could barely move the next day.'

Rounding out and perfectly balancing the acting extremes of Willis and Pitt was Madeleine Stowe, one of Hollywood's finest and most undervalued assets, in the pivotal grounding role of Dr Kathryn Railly. Gilliam had met Stowe while casting for *A Tale of Two Cities* and was immediately impressed with her charm, humour, intelligence – and hands. 'There are two things that are surprising about her – her hands are really like workers' hands, although her face is so beautiful and ethereal, and she's got this incredible horse laugh,' remarks Gilliam. 'You have few opportunities in life to work with somebody like Terry,' said Stowe. 'There aren't many directors who are as stunning as he is in their approach. Terry doesn't like to follow the expected course of things.'

SEARCHING FOR HOP

AD 1996-1997
Guardian

VIRUS MUTATING
THE LAST DAYS OF
MANKIND
ow that this mysterious
us has been isolated
a scientists
a cure?

d reaches 5 billion

With his cast in place, Gilliam then set out to find his locations. David and Janet Peoples had originally set their screenplay between Philadelphia and Baltimore, although between them they had never visited either city. Gilliam toyed with a number of alternatives, including L.A. and New York, and even at one point, London, going as far as scouting some potential locations. Wisely, he went back to the script. The locations in *Twelve Monkeys* are as key to the telling of the tale as the skyscraping locale of *Fisher King*. Philadelphia was the birthplace of America and home of the Liberty Bell. That the future denizens of *Twelve Monkeys* should be struggling for rebirth in the very cradle of their former glorious nation was perfectly appropriate.

'Sitting in England, I always thought I was commenting on America, but in a much more abstract, oblique way. But now I could just do it, boom, direct. And there was something about being in Philadelphia – the City of Brotherly Love, the Liberty Bell [also the Python musical theme] – all that is there. The old part of the city is very English-looking, with great Georgian townhouses, then you move into the American part of the city. It's like a dartboard because there is the old money out there in the green, outside the city, then you get into the next ring and it's all black. Then you get into the centre of town and it's the corporations and they're white, then you get to the City Hall and all the City Hall workers are black, then you get to the mayor's office and he's white. So it's like this amazing target. It is this strange, split place, which was perfect for the movie.'

Armed with video camera and Polaroid, Gilliam scouted a variety of locations in the two cities, settling on a number of abandoned power stations, which became home to Cole's oppressive future world. As with other projects, the locations Gilliam discovered shaped the design of the movie. 'That's the good thing about Philadelphia and Baltimore. These are former industrial cities where the industry has all left. In Philadelphia there are two or three huge power stations left standing. because there's no need for the power. So we had access to these places and in one there was a huge turbine with a face which had a hole in the middle of it, and I said "That's great, that's where you put a body," so it became the time machine. Then we put him in this cocoon. It was like amniotic sacs, cocoons, larvae, and he's naked in there – all these things are images you just start working on.'

In many of Gilliam's movies there is, he is proud to say, a wall that tells the whole story of the movie, whether it is Kevin's bedroom montage in *Time Bandits* or Parry's basement shrine full of Red Knights and pictures of Lydia in *The Fisher King*. In *Twelve Monkeys*, the wall is the engineer's room, densely covered in newspaper clippings and images.

Filming on location went smoothly, although Gilliam referred to it at the time as 'the most unenjoyable film-making experience I've ever had.' This was, in part, a reference to the difficulty for all concerned to keep track of the film's varied time patterns while filming out of sequence. On certain days, Gilliam would find himself confiding in Stowe, both of them trying to work out where they actually were in the script.

La Jetee had referenced Hitchcock's *Vertigo*, something that the Peoples had incorporated into their script, but as Gilliam shaped those scenes in his film, he began to think that the 'movie gods' were on hand. 'Madeleine coming out with the blonde wig was not planned. In the script the girl is blonde and she wears a black wig. Madeleine had dark hair so we had to give her a blonde wig, and when we started shooting that sequence I said, "Fuck this, this is ridiculous. The Hitchcock blonde has arrived." But that was not something that was scripted or planned, it was just a case of hiring Madeleine. Then it got even more bizarre because the editor Mick Audsley grabbed some music off the soundtrack of *Vertigo*, and we needed to find where it came from in the film so we could credit it properly. I found where it came from: the scene when the brown-haired Kim Novak comes out looking like the blonde Kim Novak. We were playing it on the video and then we looked at where we had put it on our film – and it's exactly that scene. It's the moment she comes out and Jimmy Stewart looks at her, and the moment Madeleine comes out and Bruce looks at her. And it's cut exactly the same way, and it's not planned. But the whole thing is cut almost shot for shot. And then it gets even more ridiculous because what we didn't use, but I shot, is the scene where they actually kiss. I shot from a platform with them kissing and the whole room spinning around them. And that's what happens in *Vertigo*. It just got so fucking bizarre. And at these moments you think something is going on here. There are forces and I don't know what those forces are. The scene originally was them going off to a back room for a quick shag, and I wanted something more poetic, and the foyer they were in was round so we did this wonderful sweeping thing. Had I left it in, people would have said we'd lifted the complete sequence from *Vertigo*.'

Twelve Monkeys mixed Gilliam themes with some of Hollywood's biggest stars to startling effect. It's a time-travel movie that may simply be a prolonged psychotic episode, a slice of pre-millennial tension rooted in the fears of our age. AIDS plays its part visually and thematically, with both Willis's 'human condom' bodysuit and the inevitability of the virus that has wiped out mankind. For all of Gilliam's dabblings in science fiction, *Twelve Monkeys* is actually his only future vision on film, *Brazil* only being presumed to be such. In common with *Brazil*, the view is a disturbing, dystopian one. 'They're living in a submarine; they're living in a mine. You don't have open, free, jolly societies in those places because it's about survival. People kept saying it's totalitarian. I don't think it is; it's just autocratic. They have very tough rules and that's the problem with Cole – ultimately he's not a very good soldier. He's got frailties, like falling in love and sensitivity, and there's a price to pay for that.'

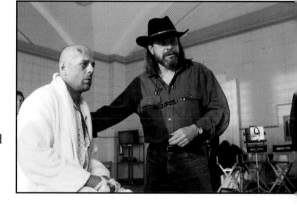

Twelve Monkeys opened during the Christmas season of 1995 at the number one spot at the American box office, where it remained for a number of weeks. It earned over $60 million in the U.S. alone before repeating the success overseas. Once again, Gilliam had delivered a studio movie that managed to work on both their terms and his. On their terms, the film made money and landed Brad Pitt an Academy Award nomination. On Gilliam's terms, it confounded expectation in a provocative, dazzling way. At once his most 'serious'

film to date, *Twelve Monkeys* was in a strange way his least personal. The film did, however, provide him with another opportunity to examine his homeland, from the point of view of an almost alien mentality. The character of Cole in his quest is in many ways a reflection of the director: he is someone both separate and separated from the world he visits and in love with the memories of his childhood, unconsciously measuring them against the reality of the 'here and now'. 'I think I started doing what Antonioni did when he came to England when he made *Blow Up*,' says the filmmaker. 'Suddenly I'm a foreigner looking at America again. But I'm a weird foreigner.'

BOB McCABE: *Twelve Monkeys* was your second Hollywood film and your second movie as 'director for hire'. What lured you in?
TERRY GILLIAM: It had this thing about whether the

central character was mad or not. Has he come back from the future to find this virus, as he claims, or is he one more apocalyptic nut? I liked the idea of a guy coming back from a very regimented society to our world and seeing what a messy, complex, chaotic place it is. What was interesting was these two Hollywood films [*The Fisher King* and *Twelve Monkeys*] were the easiest of any films I'd ever done. I think that's a result of the other films — basically of being a troublemaker and having proved that I care about what I'm doing and I don't suffer executives very easily. They all seem to understand that I'm very serious about what I make and I will kill all who get in the way, so basically that keeps a lot of people away from me.

BM: How much of the design was in the script?
TG: None of it. The script just said they were underground. It's what you choose to show. Once you're underground, it seemed to me you'd be obsessed by your air-filtration systems — that's why those valves were big like that. We had lots of discussions, and then I said, ultimately, that in some ways you don't want to see too much. I wanted to keep it vague enough that it could just be a product of his deranged mind. To me the trick was to try and make it feel like he was mad. We didn't want to believe that he's from the future.

BM: How compatible were Willis and Pitt as performers?
TG: It was really interesting to watch Bruce. He became like the old gunfighter and the new boy's in town, and rather than being threatened by him, he took him under his wing. Maybe he was threatened by him, but the way he dealt with it was by not pushing him away but by embracing him. The crew really liked Brad, and Bruce really likes to be liked. Normally he wouldn't hang around the set — he'd come in and do his stuff and go out. But when Brad was there, Bruce started hanging around the set, and it got very jolly at that time. If there was competitiveness there, it came out in a really good way, supporting each other. And there was one day when Brad lost it totally and Bruce was really good at trying to help him, rather than gloating. It brought out the best in Bruce, frankly. He went for it and it was great.

The spectrum of acting is very broad in that film and Bruce and Brad are at opposite ends of the spectrum, and Madeleine is right in the middle. It's a thing that I think I keep getting criticised for, being too grabby and too greedy to go from here to there all in one movie. It throws a lot of people, but that's what I liked about it and it makes me happy. I like them both. I think Brad's really funny and really believable and Bruce grows the more you watch it — it's a really subtle performance. It's like he's totally naked, totally vulnerable. There's none of Bruce Willis's defensive cleverness, because he is a very defensive guy in that sense. I remember showing him the scene in the hotel room with Madeleine, and he watched it and said "Jesus, I don't have to do anything." I said, "That's right, that's what's great." And I think he was very impressed with himself and frightened at the same time. Working with him was hard because I couldn't push back and Bruce likes pushing. It's the way he works. I wanted to kill him half the time, but I could never push him back because we'd get into a pushing contest and I didn't want the character to have anything to push against. It drove me crazy because I had no outlet.

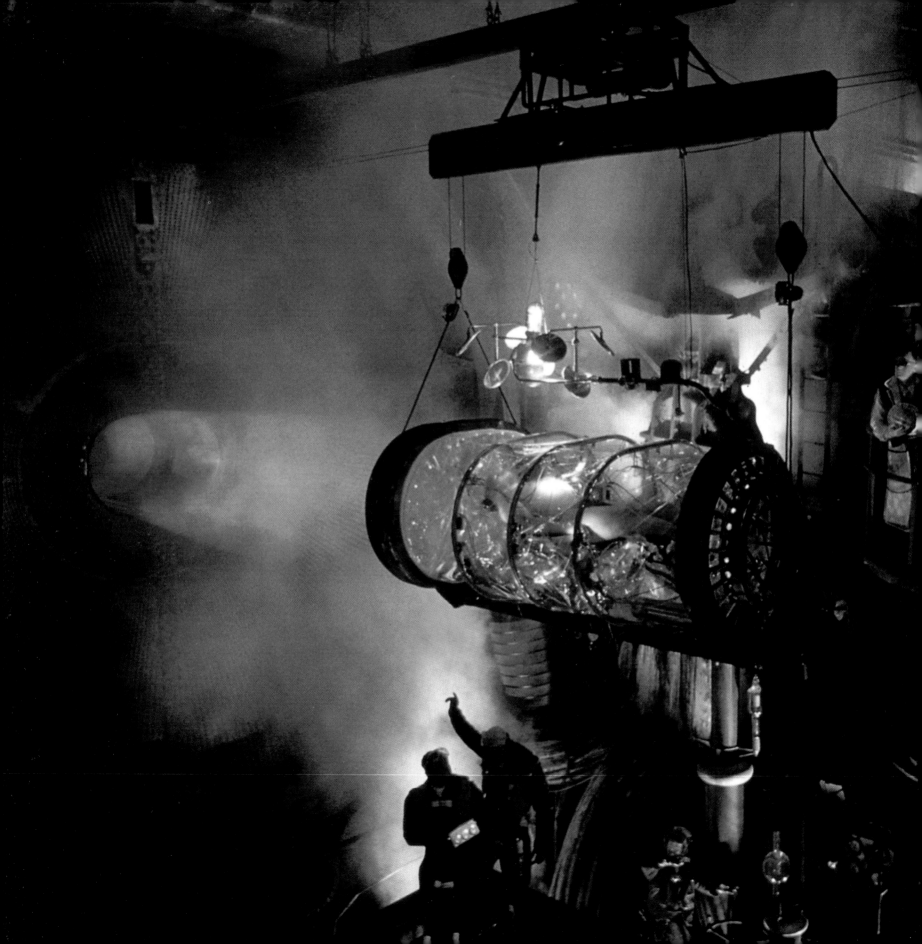

BM: There are certain connections to *Fisher King* in the themes of homelessness and AIDS again, and the look of the hospital scenes.

TG: That stuff is still in my head. I keep thinking I'm doing these leaps but maybe it's just a steady progression. The hospital definitely, and the madness in there is like *Fisher King*. I'm aware that they do connect, but not consciously. That hospital was actually a prison which was built in a hub shape. You've got the hub and the spokes going out wheel-shaped. That one room which we used was three passages going off and I thought it was fantastic. I wanted to use just that room, but the way I justified it is that his mind is trifurcated. It's a schizophrenic mind, and the room is schizophrenic. I can never work out how this process works, except that if my gut says use it, it's really good. I think I'm still living in Dickensian times. Bedlam rears its ugly head. The closest I've got to getting away from that was in *Brazil*, but even that has an antique feel to it. The funny thing about the hospital we used in *The Fisher King* is that it was a disused warehouse for nuts — a nut house. So I can't run from those bad puns.

BM: AIDS and the notion of a killer virus provides an undercurrent in the movie, with Cole's suit having been termed a 'human condom'.

TG: Very much. None of that was in the script. I just got into the human condom thing. There was a logic, it seemed to me, in that what the movie became about was how people isolate themselves from one another, through latex or the video ball. I love that moment, again something I put in, when Cole and Kathryn are on the run and the cop car comes by and they turn away from the cop car, and there they are up on all those video screens. That was about video and television as another form of separation between people, an electronic condom.

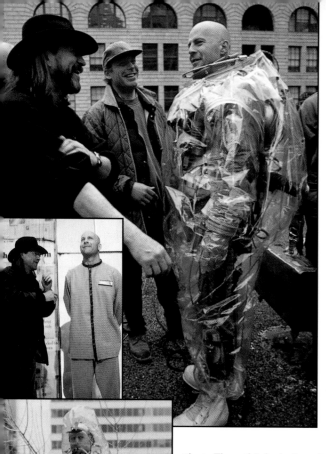

BM: What parameters do you set out when making a time-travel movie?

TG: If your going back in time has always been predetermined, then you have always been there. You don't have a choice in the matter. You might think you have a choice, but you're going to go back in time and you will be part of that event. I think *Twelve Monkeys* is very Oriental in that sense — that's why I did the wheel of the monkeys going round for the poster design. It's trying to break out of it, but it's a wheel that keeps going round. And that's one of the things that attracted me to it, that the kid is always going to see himself die. Then he's going to grow up and the world is going to be decimated, he's going to break the law and end up in prison, and it's going to go on and on and on. Just this wheel turning and turning. It has this predestination. People get very weird about the female scientist being there at the end — she has come back. Cole says it earlier: 'Once I've found out what it is, they will send scientists back to get the virus.' So she's come back. He's done his job. Five billion are still going to die. It's all going to go on and on and on. The people in the future aren't interested in stopping it. They are only interested in getting the virus so that they can develop an antidote, so that they can reclaim the planet. Five billion are going to die and they are always going to die. That to me was an important part of why I wanted to do it. And the Americans in particular had a hard time accepting that. They think she's going to save the day. They're doomed. Originally, what David and Jan had were more people going through time, and I hope this connection works. Madeleine's character is talking about this medieval preacher in her lecture and on the street, when they are on the run, there is that guy preaching. Well, it's the same guy. Half the prophets were obviously people being sent back from the future when their machinery wasn't working properly and sending them back to old testament times. I thought that was very smart.

BM: Obviously the chance to explore madness in all its various forms in this movie appealed to you, but there is an interesting thing about madness here in that it almost becomes a virus itself, in that it shifts between people — Cole's psychosis becomes Kathryn's, if it is in fact psychosis.

TG: The thing with madness normally is its intensity and its belief. If you believe something strongly enough, others tend to think maybe you're right, because most people are uncertain about everything, and I find that's how Hollywood works. It's full of all these neurotic, uncertain, desperate people who

are making huge amounts of money, and their job is to try and make you as neurotic as them. I find that, ultimately, if I stand still long enough in Hollywood, they start circling around me because I'm the only thing standing still. I don't have a problem with madness. I go out to Hollywood and it's nothing but madness, and the most successful people are the most mad people. The only people who

(Clockwise, from above) The poster used; Gilliam's end of shoot sketch; two alternative Gilliam posters; the wrap party invite; another unused poster concept

aren't crazy are the ones who get on and do their normal little jobs. They may go psychotic, but they're not crazy people. I think Hollywood is a continual form of madness.

BM: You consciously didn't use many storyboards on this one.

TG: I used a couple for the early stuff, and some of the scenes with the animals because they were special effects. But with *Fisher King* I got rid of storyboards pretty much, and the same thing here. I just didn't want to use them. I wanted to let the actors dictate, let the scene dictate, what happens. It is partly me getting more confident, and partly you end up looking at them [storyboards] and not looking at what's in front of you. It's trying to learn to see properly — see what is there and not what you've pre-planned. I'm just trying to loosen it up.

BM: The last sequence is amazingly complex in that you have the past, the present and the future all converging in the one place, and then drawing in this tragedy, seen through various people's eyes at various times.

TG: We shot a lot of stuff and we put it together. You know what the shots are. We tried various slow motion and stuff. There is all sorts of stuff that's cut out of that. I think with film you write it, you're convinced this is the way to do it, then you shoot it, and then you cut the shit out of it. And everybody does it, that's the process. I'd be very curious to see who doesn't do it that way — who actually is able to see a film so clearly when they set out that they shoot what is going to end up as the final cut. I think Hitchcock convinced everybody that's what he did, and I'm really curious if that's what he really did. And we all then had to live up to his lie, I guess. What I'm always finding is how I can do it with less — there was a look, there was a move, that suddenly captured it.

TWELVE MONKEYS
WRAP PARTY

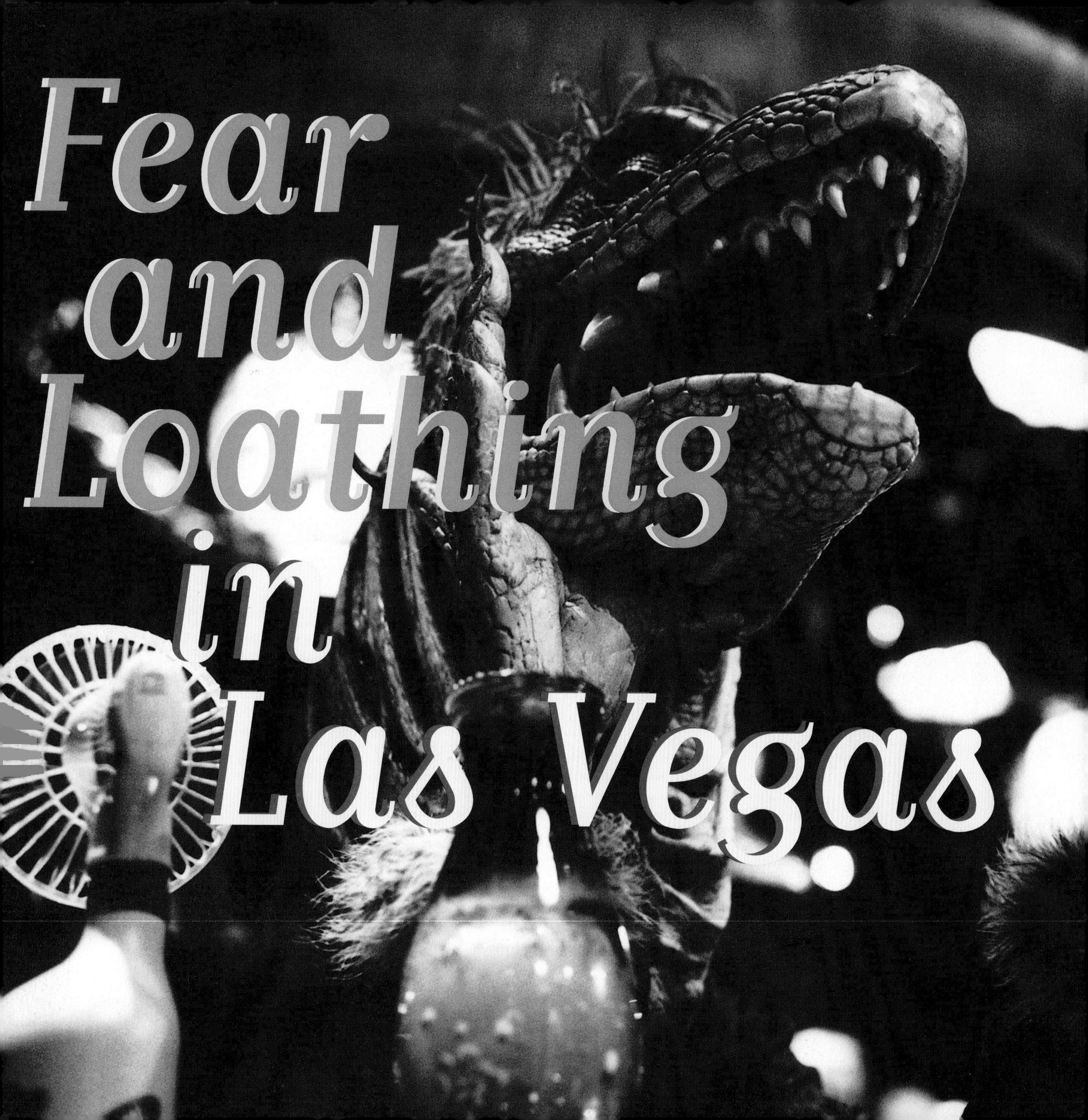
Fear
and
Loathing
in
Las Vegas

'MY GUESS IS THAT TODAY'S AUDIENCE wants this film desperately. I think they need it. That's why I've been referring to *Fear and Loathing* as a cinematic enema for the 1990s — just clean out the system. There's a lot of shame attached to this movie, and we're all very sorry. We want to apologise in advance for whatever it is we've done.' Terry Gilliam, on the set of *Fear and Loathing in Las Vegas*, 1997.

Terry Gilliam decamped from Los Angeles during the 'Summer of Love' in 1967, before anyone had got around to coining the phrase. Hunter S. Thompson stuck with America, up the coast in San Francisco, but by the dawn of the 1970s, Thompson was also beginning to see the cracks. Gilliam took it personally; Thompson took it nationally. Maybe it was the times, maybe it was his mind, maybe it was the vast amounts of drugs and alcohol, or maybe – perhaps more than anything — the timing was right. Either way, the sometime sports journalist Thompson took a standard assignment to cover the Mint 400 off-road race outside of Las Vegas and turned it into one of the most eloquent, excessive, erratic and wonderful decimations and examinations of a nation ever committed to paper. In Thompson's prose, he sought not only to tell the American public that the American Dream was dead, but to explain where it died, how it bit the big one, what it's last words were and why an ether-crazed doctor of journalism and his somewhat disoriented Samoan attorney were the only ones to show up (or wise up) to the funeral. The result was a serialisation in *Rolling Stone* that led to the book *Fear and Loathing in Las Vegas*. The phrase 'fear and loathing' entered the lexicon, while the book itself entered the minds of countless people across the globe. The idealism of the 1960s was laid to waste by a combination of Charles Manson, Altamont, the Beatles splitting up, Vietnam escalating to insane proportions and Richard Nixon being re-elected by appearing on *Rowan and Martin's Laugh In*. These were the images and the events; Thompson put it all into words.

Converting the book back into images via film was inevitable. A Hollywood reinvigorated by the unexpected 'youth' successes of *The Graduate* and *Easy Rider* struggled for years to bring Thompson's vision to the screen. Jack Nicholson was involved at one point; hell, everyone was involved at one point, but no one could crack it. Not even Terry Gilliam, who occasionally found an adaptation landing on his desk, generally when he was busy on something else. In the days after *Munchausen*, his good friend and Thompson illustrator Ralph Steadman urged Terry Gilliam to make the film. But in the end, the job fell to Alex Cox, the director of *Repo Man* and *Sid and Nancy*.

Hunter S. Thompson lives in Woody Creek, Colorado, shoots guns, and suffers fools not terribly gladly. Despite having won approval from Thompson associate and producer Laila Nabulsi, Cox was barely suffered at all. 'He went up to Hunter's house and completely alienated Hunter in one fell swoop,' claims Gilliam.

'Cox had a vision of the film that was off; it was wrong,' explains Johnny Depp, who was already cast in the role of Raoul Duke and had spent many preparatory months hanging out with Thompson. Depp became Thompson's road manager for a book tour and even ended up locked in a San Francisco hotel room with Thompson for five days straight. He recounts of the time, 'We had seventy five salt and pepper shakers, a tuna salad from three days ago, which we can't throw out because you never know when you'll need it, bucket after bucket of ice, a lot of Chivas Regal.'

'Cox had this great material to work with, and he took it and he added his own stuff to it,' continues Depp, 'which was not good. He had this literal version of the "wave" speech, when I'm talking about San Francisco in the mid-1960s – this beautiful, profound section of the book and the movie. And Cox's literal approach to it was a cartoon of Raoul Duke riding the crest of a wave across the desert. It was wrong, really bad. Alex had a difficult time understanding that Hunter Thompson is the real visionary here. And as long as you can recognise that, then you can apply your own vision to it. Cox has an unfortunate ego on him, and his approach to Hunter was bad. He was condescending. He thought because, maybe, Hunter's drunk, I can slide one past him, but Hunter just ate him alive, just eviscerated him, verbally destroyed him.'

Depp was signed for the project before anyone, and fondly recalled his first meeting with Thompson. 'We built a bomb in his kitchen and took it out to his backyard and he handed me a nickel-plated 12 gauge shotgun, and I fired at the bomb and there was an eighty-foot fireball. That was my first meeting with him. We're both from Kentucky, so there was this kind of homeboy thing. My goal was to steal his soul. To absorb as much of him as I could.' Another actor to play Thompson on screen also had a taste of Thompson's outrageous behaviour. Bill Murray, who portrayed a watered-down version of the good doctor in the 1980 film *Where the Buffalo Roam*, reportedly urinated with Thompson in a hotel lobby.

Terry Gilliam, meanwhile, was facing a beast of his own fancy – the minotaur. Working with British screenwriter Tony Grisoni, who had penned Jon Amiel's delightful, but little seen, *Queen of Hearts*, Gilliam had resurrected his tale of the Greek warrior Theseus, a long-held ambition that, at one point, had Michael Palin pencilled in to co-write. Hearing that Alex Cox was attached to the project, Tony Grisoni had offered his services as screenwriter. While Gilliam and family were enjoying their customary month-long sojourn in their ruins of an Italian castle, Terry was offered *Fear and Loathing*. By the time Gilliam returned to the U.K. Cox was out and he was in, and Grisoni's fondness for the project led to a natural collaboration on the screenplay.

'The minute Terry Gilliam came into the picture, it turned from being a Cessna plane to a 747,' says actor Benecio Del Toro, by now signed to play the role of Dr Gonzo. 'It just turned into "here we go". The way Terry approached the work is the right way for this film.' In near homage to the book, Gilliam and Grisoni shut the doors, battened down the hatches, got out the magic markers and banged out a first draft of the screenplay in eight days. On the ninth day they rested. On the tenth they realised they needed a re-write. 'I think we just missed the tone of certain things to be honest,' says Gilliam. 'We got all this stuff in there, but it isn't it, it isn't right. So we started chopping and changing and it wasn't major stuff, but the thing is so much about tone, you just get one thing wrong and suddenly you're off in the wrong direction. It feels that way to me.'

'When we sat down to adapt it, we were literally side by side at the computer,' adds co-scripter Grisoni, 'and we did it very fast, the first draft. Whenever we needed a line of dialogue, we would look to the book and pick it from another part of the book and put it where we wanted. We avoided inventing dialogue ourselves. The stage directions were also 90% taken from the book. So our job became one of collage. The meat was, and will always be, Hunter Thompson's. We cannibalised and used bits from here and there, but the main problem was, for a two hour movie, you've got to give it a shape. As far as the run of scenes went, we stuck pretty close to the book for the first part, and then further developed things that were already happening in the book. It was a matter of bringing these things out more.'

'If you're gonna do a book, you've got to try and do the book,' Gilliam says. 'I find it very difficult to take a book and, especially when the people are still living like Ralph Steadman being a friend and Hunter is out there, you don't wanna just say "this is

mine." I think what they wrote is like music. They wrote the symphony, and I'm the conductor now with a new group and I actually change the arrangement. That's kind of what it's like.'

Gilliam's American movies had proven an interesting journey back to reality for the filmmaker. Having made a remarkable trilogy of films in England that celebrated and defended to the death (or at least to madness) the power and wonder of fantasy over reality, with *The Fisher King*, Gilliam and his characters faced up to reality. Parry escaped into madness; Jack walked away from his existence. With Parry's simple line 'Can I miss her now?' he brought a level of reality crashing into both *Fisher King* and Gilliam's cannon as a whole. Here was a film that came out the other side of the looking glass, that reflected back from the real world.

With *Twelve Monkeys*, Gilliam presented a character that was sent to study, impartially, what had gone wrong in the recent history of his once glorious country. Cole could have just as easily been a Woodward or Bernstein as an emissary from a bug-guzzling future vision of ourselves. In *Twelve Monkeys* the characters longed for madness, to believe that all of the knowledge they carried of the modern world and the world to come was a psychotic delusion. But it wasn't. Gilliam was finding that 'you won't get far on hot air and fantasy' in America, and here in these two films was reality, distilled through some remarkable visions.

Fear and Loathing represented even more of a homecoming for Gilliam than *Fisher King*. It was the movie that brought him back not only to his home country, but to the era and the sentiment that had led to his self-imposed exile. As Gilliam points out himself, he has now spent more time in England than America. His family is English, and he was mildly miffed to be awarded Best Director *outside* of the Best British Director category at the 1996 *Empire* magazine awards. Although he never had a burning desire to go home, there was obviously a need to explore what had made him leave. Thompson's tome gave him that chance. If the American dream was dead, then surely it should be the mad people – the Thompsons, the Gilliams – that got to dance on its grave. That was the appeal to Gilliam of the apparently 'unfilmable' *Fear and Loathing*.

The film became a very personal experience for Gilliam. Where Thompson stayed, Gilliam had left. 'The beginning was a definite rebellion. Having left the place, I didn't want to have anything to do with America, even though I always said my films were "messages in bottles" floated back across the ocean. They were always about America, but heavily disguised. *Brazil* was, for

*Director Gilliam and star
Depp on set, 1997*

me, about my experience with bureaucracy in America. *Jabberwocky* was this idea of a Midwest used car salesman. Even though they're American films, the perspective is different from what it would've been had I lived and worked in America. I suppose with *Fear and Loathing* I'm really going back to search for the American Dream. I'm really going back to the heart of the whole thing, and I am more at ease with it. I'm less threatened by America. What's so strange about coming back to it though, is that, when we were shooting this film, I was out for six or seven months and I couldn't wait to get back to England. I can be quite content out there, but I can't wait to get back here because I find the ground is shifting under your feet out there. There's no ground: it's sand sprinkled on the surface every day, fresh. And each day is a new day and history began that morning when you woke up. People ask if I could ever go back there? No, I could never go back and live there. I get enough of it in these little jaunts to make movies, but I can't get the American out of me basically. It's always there, and I like the fact that it's created this hybrid creature which is me, which is neither one or the other. It helps me keep this different perspective.'

Fear and Loathing in Las Vegas, the movie, hit 'the strip' in August of 1997. It would be nice to say that Vegas was never the same afterwards, but Vegas is a law unto itself. There is no coincidence that Hunter Thompson sought to find the American

Dream in the shallowest of cities, or that once again Gilliam found himself capturing one of the most familiar and symbolic of American locales.

'I think it's all there, but unconsciously. You look at New York, but it's not America, and Philadelphia is what America lost, after the war when industry moved west. With both *Fisher King* and *Fear and Loathing*, I've ended up shooting half the film in L.A. so I'm stuck in a place that's also America, but it isn't. Nobody could have ever invented Hollywood – this whole dream factory full of people who are completely out of touch with reality and America, yet they create the dreams that Americans think *are* America, and people live their lives trying to emulate what they see on the screen. It's bizarre.'

The director had planned to populate his film with a number of star names in supporting roles. 'I wanted to get all the old guys from the 1960s. I mean, Nicholson, Hopper, Fonda, to be in there. In the end we mainly got the young brood – Christina Ricci, and Cameron Diaz and Toby Maguire and then we got people like Lyle Lovett, and Harry Dean Stanton was the oldest one, and Ellen Barkin, Gary Busey, Katherine Helmond, Mark Harmon. People just wanted to be part of this thing and they all worked for scale, which is great, and so they would come in to do their one day's appearance and have a nice little scene.'

Johnny Depp shaved his head for the movie and Benicio Del Toro gained around 40 pounds. Del Toro also began shooting by becoming ill. 'I got sick in Vegas,' the actor recalls. 'I had a cold and fever on the first day of shooting, and just trying to find medicine in that town is impossible. You get into an elevator, and it's crowded. The lights are everywhere, and the sound of the casino. And you walk outside and it's hot, and there's sprinklers hitting you, and you don't know if there's a pharmacy anywhere.'

Fear and Loathing in Las Vegas, budgeted for less than $19 million, was shot on a tight fifty-six day schedule, with filming taking place in Las Vegas itself for the first two and a half weeks and the last two, and studio time in L.A. in between. 'I thought to myself, "We're making a dangerous film here",' said Gilliam, 'and I'm supposed to be pretending to be a young filmmaker again and taking chances, so why not?'

In recreating the Vegas of the 1970s (all rear projection shots were lifted from the old Robert Urich TV show, *Vegas*), several institutions refused to extend a welcome to the production. Already under a tight schedule, this necessitated the building of numerous sets and the changing of many location names. As the screenplay progressed, Gilliam had begun to flesh out Thompson's words with inventive and unusual visuals. For a man relatively inexperienced in the ways of drugs, most agreed Gilliam, with his creeping carpet designs, was getting it right. As Depp put it: 'This is a guy who understands acid trips without ever having taken acid.'

Gilliam employed a number of devices in creating this off-kilter view of the world, including dropping frames from certain shots to create a disjointed effect for the viewer. 'It's probably not accurate to the drugs,' says the director, 'but my sense of drugs to me has always been about how your perception changes.' Animatronics expert Rob Bottin was called in to provide the occupants of the lizard lounge sequence, while Peerless Camera added to the overall effect.

'It started off fairly light in terms of FX stuff,' explains Ken Houston. 'A lot of my contemporaries said I would have a lot of fun doing all the psychedelic stuff, but Terry didn't take that approach. The most complicated shot was the lizard lounge because it hadn't been planned as an FX shot. There was a problem filling the bar, so we had to work out a way to do a split screen effect with a moving camera. What complicated it was that the bar was mirrored, and wherever you looked there were reflections. So I had to use a computer-controlled camera on set, and very carefully plan who went where and how to deal with the camera reflections. That shot ended up being very time-consuming. The other thing about it is the shot is a track back through the bar, which means the camera is on rails and they come into shot. So we had to find a way to eliminate those rails as well. That was a bit hair-raising.'

Having been burned by the lay-off period after *Fisher King*, Gilliam had leapt at the chance to get back behind a camera so quickly after *Twelve Monkeys*, with barely a year having elapsed between signing the deal and seeing the movie in cinemas. 'I did it partly to try and break out of the responsibility of making good films, making them well, let's put it that way. I just wanted to do something fast and Gonzo – Gonzo filmmaking is what we wanted to do. That's why the idea of a low budget and a short schedule was important. I knew once we got into it I'd start screaming and shouting very much like Duke in the book, just railing against everything, but that's the spirit of the piece, so why not go for it? The worst thing was when I did start doing it, I realised I wasn't as young as I used to be, and I don't have the energy I used to have when we did the earlier things, but we still got through it.'

Working under such pressures, Gilliam found himself unable to rely on the production company. 'Johnny [Depp] was so incensed with the production company and the guy who runs it that he said if he comes on the set, he was going to put in his contract that this guy has to drop his trousers and Johnny gets to whip him with a wire coathanger. This is how angry he was.'

Nonetheless, *Fear and Loathing* wrapped without incident. The same can not be said for post-production. With mere weeks to go before its release, the Writer's Guild of America decided that screenplay credit should go to Alex Cox and Tod Davies. The WGA's reasoning dictates that a director counts as a production executive, and therefore must prove, by their standards, to have written at least 60% of the screenplay to receive any credit. Any other writer, or team of writers, need just 33%. Given that most of the words in debate were Thompson's anyway, the argument seemed ridiculous, and Gilliam went to war with the WGA, attacking the clandestine nature of their workings and threatening to resign. He eventually won the right to have his name featured on the film he co-wrote, although Cox and Davies are also still credited. This action was still in debate a mere two weeks before the film's American release, and the whole event prompted Gilliam to make a short entitled *The Dress Pattern*. Had the WGA not reneged, this short would have opened the film, showing Ray Cooper sitting behind a desk, the American flag behind him and a framed photo of Hunter Thompson beside him, intoning: 'Ladies and gentlemen, the film you are about to see this evening is the first film ever made *not* based on a screenplay. At no time were writers involved. Efforts have been made to deny this aston-ishing, yet simple, truth by a dangerous, possibly foreign-controlled organisation, which, for reasons of national security, must remains nameless... but *do not be deceived!* Using only the finest gems from the workshop of that great American patri-ot, Dr Hunter S. Thompson, this film was hand-assembled by dedicated craftsmen working, not from a screenplay, but from an original and ingenious dress pattern designed by two fearless fighters for truth, justice and the American way – Mr Tony Grisoni and his assistant Mr Terry Gilliam. Remember Americans, *do not*... I repeat...*do not* be deceived! Your country depends on *you!* Thank you.'

The WGA backed down; *The Dress Pattern* remains unseen.

This incident was not the end of Gilliam's fights for *Fear and Loathing*. The film that Gilliam hoped would provide a 'cinematic enema for the 1990s', was booed at its Cannes Film Festival premiere and denounced by numerous critics. Other prominent critics, normally admirers of the filmmaker's work, ignored the work, seeking not to add to what quickly became a critical onslaught. Worse still, Thompson was not too happy about some slightly out-of-context comments Gilliam had made concerning him in a *New York Times* interview. 'You do not know me at all and you are not my friend,' an angry Thompson stated to Gilliam. 'You are building a very distinguished enemies list, like Nixon.'

Thompson did recant when he finally saw the movie, hailing it a masterpiece and calling it 'an eerie trumpet-call over a lost battlefield,' but there was clearly, by now, no love lost between the two men. 'If you see pictures from the New York premiere,' says Gilliam, 'you'll see pictures of Hunter, Johnny and Benicio, or Johnny, Benicio and me, but you'll never see all four of us together. When he comes out in public, he behaves like an idiot and he can't stop himself. I think he's so nervous when he's out there, and I said "OK, it's your premiere" and just walked away. We went and had several drinks while the film was on. I just wanted out of it.

'With *Fear and Loathing*,' Gilliam remarked while editing his movie, 'I keep connecting to the moment I was the head of the school safety patrol, in my sash and everything, a guardian of law and order. And this kid came running down a corridor and I was walking along with my friend and I pushed my friend in front of the kid, just to see what would happen. And I was dragged into the principal's office and he was gobsmacked, "Gilliam, how could you, what was going on?" And I got 'swats', as they were called. But it was really weird. Why did I do that? I just wanted to see what would happen. Why did I make *Fear and Loathing*? I just wanted to see what would happen.'

What happened was that *Fear and Loathing in Las Vegas* opened in the U.S. opposite Roland Emmerich's *Godzilla*, which was largely expected to be the biggest beast at the summer of 1998 box office. *Godzilla* was considered something of a flop after a domestic gross of $125 million; *Fear and Loathing* made considerably less and was tarred with the same brush. Like *Munchausen* before it, the film was a literary adaptation in which the filmmaker had found a deep, personal resonance, but which had attracted some of the most negative press in recent memory. Like *Munchasuen* before it, the film was deemed a failure because of its lack of box office performance, but it was a complex film that demanded more of an audience than most mainstream fare. While at times gloriously erratic, the movie was a major artistic triumph for Gilliam.

For years people said *Fear and Loathing* was unfilmable. But the reality proved that what was filmable could be unpleasant. Gilliam's film takes the audience into a room with two men who are, for the most part, out of their heads. One of them happens to be a very good writer who, through

drug-induced mayhem and confusion, finds something worthy to say, but the audience has to go through that mayhem and confusion to get to it. That is the point. Hunter Thompson's book put a motel room in the reader's mind that was populated by two, ultimately, iconic figures. Terry Gilliam's movie puts the viewer right in that room, right at that moment. For anyone who has ever been stuck in a room with someone out of their head – whether they are a respected 'doctor' of journalism or not – it is not always a pleasant place to be. But that is why the movie is correct in its approach. The end result offers a candid reality – the unfilmable filmed. The fact that most people watching the movie would not want to star in it is exactly the way it should be. In 1998, working within the Hollywood system, Terry Gilliam made a *difficult* film. The feeling that evokes is, sadly, already a distant memory. But no, it is more than that. Hell, it's an 'eerie trumpet call over a lost battlefield'.

BOB McCABE: What was your initial response to making *Fear and Loathing* after all these years?

TERRY GILLIAM: A lot of people kept saying 'You've gotta update it, to make it relevant to the 1990s.' I don't think you have to make it relevant, it's relevant whenever. Two people going to excess is basically what it's about, and the excuse for this behaviour, on some level, is the loss of the dream of the 1960s, and the continuing war and all of that, which is, it seems to me, underneath everything in that book.

I remember when I read the Cox script, which got me involved in this thing, it started out brilliantly. I was laughing because it was just straight from the book, but then it just had no form to it, no shape with no underlying story going on there, and it just became boorish and tiresome. So one of the main things that we tried to do was to make sure you cared about those characters. We were very clear in our thinking. We decided it was like Dante's *Inferno*, and Gonzo was a kind of Virgil, but he wasn't a poet, he was this force hell-bent on death and destruction. He was like some pagan elemental primal thing that was out of control half the time. Then you had Duke, who was Dante going along watching this and then being guided. So we're getting into this whole thing about Christianity and paganism. Like when they're on adrenachrome, Gonzo becomes like the great god Pan with his horns, and Duke has got a strange kind of Christian morality underneath all that. He is sent to hell to endure self-inflicted suffering for the sins of America.

BM: Duke is very much a conscience figure in the book, albeit an irresponsible conscience figure.

TG: Yeah, I think he is, That's the whole point of the Dr Johnson quote at the beginning: 'He who makes a beast of himself, gets rid of the pain of being a man.' You read Thompson's stuff, he's from Kentucky and the Bible is floating around there somewhere, and his references are almost biblical at times. He hides them; he ducks and dives.

What is interesting in the writing is that I find he equivocates all the time. He never takes a real stance. Even the 'wave' speech, which I think is beautiful, we made more unequivocal than he does. The book's a lot of fabrication and cheating. The Gonzo in the bath-tub scene was really him in the bath-tub, and some of the stuff with Gonzo and the girls was him, but he was married at the time and so he disguised all this. One of the ideas we were playing with was the idea that he didn't go to Vietnam, that he's a journalist but he didn't cover the war. So what he's doing by taking drugs, he is creating a war zone in his head, bombarding his psyche with drugs. And then he goes into Vegas, basically a mundane, banal place, and reports as if he was a war correspondent.

BM: The first cut I saw of the movie featured a car-top coconut-smashing scene that Johnny Depp had discovered filed away in Thompson's basement, which was eventually cut from the movie. Was there much else excised?

TG: We cut three major scenes out of the film, including that one. The others were the scene from the book where they talk to the DA from Georgia in the bar, which was great and worked a treat, but we cut it out. The other one is the big speech in the tent of the Mint 400, when the Hoodlum comes in and he goes, 'great to be here at the Mint 400, I was with my old lady and started slapping her around,' blah, blah, blah. It's a really wonderful speech but certain things just don't work as well. The film has its own momentum and you've just got to keep going at certain points.

BM: The protagonist in your movies is often related to yourself. I wasn't sure what part of Thompson you related to, but what you seem to have done is cast yourself in a similar kind of situation to the characters, outside the movie — Gonzo filmmaking and all.

TG: The making of the movie is the same as the movie. Somehow, there's always a connection between the making of it and what it's about. So this was, just go for it, just go in there and leap off the edge of the precipice and see what happens. And it's hellish. It's all the things the book says it is. It's awful, and you end up hating and screaming, and at the same time having great times too.

  It was the most uncertain experience I've had for a long time and that was part of what I was trying to do. Because normally with the films, I know them so deeply before I start shooting, I feel I could shoot blindfolded and somehow I'll get it. This one I was never quite certain of. Lesley Walker, the editor, has never seen me so uncertain about things, and it's partly because I'm feeling my way through this thing. I also wanted to keep a distance to it. I didn't want to like the film; I didn't want to love it. I wanted to maintain this objectivity, because I didn't know what we were really ultimately going to make. Whereas normally in my films I feel I know the rhythm of the film when I'm making it.

BM: Do you think your lack of drug experience helped the movie?

TG: I don't know because everything I was doing I just did instinctively. I mean I didn't do any research to find out about the effect of mescaline and acid. It was only afterwards that Johnny was watching it and said, 'Jesus that's just like acid.' Like on *Fisher King*, I didn't do any study of mental illness, but it felt right. Then, later, a lot of people who have been down those paths and who had those kind of experiences said, 'you've got it spot on.' I just think probably I'm that close to madness, whether it's drug-induced or not, and I can feel where it should go. I mean, I did want, at the end of this whole thing, to take some hallucinogenic drugs just to complete the whole thing. You know, twenty five years later to round it out with that, but I keep not getting time to do it! I never took acid when I was living in L.A. because I was living in this glass house up on stilts in Laurel Canyon, and I just knew I'd fly, I'd go right out the windows. I mean I almost wanted to do it without any acid. That's why I stayed away from a lot of drugs, because I was so close to everything. Everybody was describing to me their experiences, anyway. Things like marijuana, hash, actually make me implode, I don't really like it because I can feel myself turning inside out. I become a human black hole, and cocaine was only useful when you got off trips from London to L.A. and you get there in the late afternoon, and then the evening would go on. That was in the 1980s when coke was everywhere, and so you dabble. But I found the hangover from coke was just awful — it would last me three days just from a little snort. So I stayed away from the stuff. It's weird because I can actually say this film was made by a two-legged drug-free zone. I don't know anything about drugs.

Wouldn't you rather party with these lizards this Memorial Day?

Gilliam and Depp at the Fear & Loathing *bar. (right) Hunter S. Thompson visits the set*

BM: The film is set in 1971, but it's very much a film about the 1960s.
TG: Their behaviour is 1960s behaviour gone mad, basically. I feel it's time for that in the 1990s. What's good about it is that their behaviour, for all its bestiality and madness, is intelligent. They're intelligent people behaving in an outrageous way. They're not dumb people behaving badly; they're really smart people behaving badly, which is more interesting than punk shit where you're just head-banging. Also what's interesting is that in a sense the next wave to come along was punk, but that choice didn't seem as intelligent to me. It just seemed a dumber choice. I really felt that the choice that was made then was really intelligent people having a last hurrah, one last chance to just say 'fuck it.'

BM: The film very strongly seems to reflect your own feelings about America.
TG: I became disillusioned with the country because I grew up believing in the American Dream. I believed in truth, justice and the American way. I believed all those things and I took them for granted. Then as things changed and the world changed and I changed, I began to see that this is all bullshit. Then the war had brought everything to a head, and long hair brought everything to a head. And suddenly you're *Alice in Wonderland*, and you've gone through the looking glass and you're seeing it from the other side, and this is crazy. I always saw America as the Rome of the twentieth century, interfering with everything around the world, and that bothered me.

BM: So if the story of *Fear and Loathing* is you going back to look for the American Dream, what did you find?
TG: I think that America is still this very confused place. What I can see now is that it's got wonderful things that I rejected before, and really smart intelligent people, and yet an inherent dumbness that floats through the whole thing. And the dumbness is about the sheep-like quality of the nation now. I think what was the shock was to go to Vegas, the heart of the American Dream. I think Vegas is a wonderful display of America now, because it's the 'Disneyfication' of America. You see these Americans and they've all changed shape. These people didn't exist before — huge fat people, fat beyond any dream of fatness, and they walk like those little dolls that waddle. Then there's the other guys who used to be geeks and nerds, but now they've all body built so they've got these huge bodies and this huge neck and this little head that sits on top, and they walk in this really constricted way. Who are these people now? They're all shapes that never existed before, and they're all out there, hundreds of thousands of them, and they all go to Vegas with their kids and wander around gawking. Then there's Caesar's Palace, which is like this huge shopping mall done up as Pompeii in ancient Rome, with an arched sky above that changes colour with the day. You get this sanitised, infantile version of the world, and that's what I think America's become. Vegas has probably always been the prow of the ship, the figurehead, and it brings out the best and the worst. But there's some kind of truth there — and it's the fastest growing city in America.

Coming

IN THE WAKE OF *Fear and Loathing*, Terry Gilliam assessed his next move and found himself perusing five projects that still may see the light of day.

Theseus and the Minotaur

The first project Gilliam considered for filming was *Theseus and the Minotaur*. 'It's really about the rise and fall of civilisation, with a lot of blood and magic.' Gilliam explains. 'I am trying to do something that's not of this time. I look at primitive dances and things, and say "that's where we're going". It's about the American version of heroism. A guy starts out and does all these heroic deeds, righting wrongs and protecting the innocent, then as he moves on, things get more complex and those simple distinctions get lost. Then he gets really lost and ends up having to destroy something, and becomes a hero to the rest of the world by doing the one thing that he said he would never do. So it's about getting caught in those traps.'

Gilliam started working on the project with Tony Grisoni back in 1996, prior to *Fear and Loathing*. 'It's huge,' Grisoni enthuses of the project. 'It goes from a sort of mountainside rural setting, and then follows Theseus as he comes down and goes into a larger hill settlement, then a town, then a city, then another city. So he goes through a sort of history of civilisation, and things become more and more sophisticated around him. Terry went to look at some locations in India at one point, and I was in India last year and looked at the same locations, which would certainly work very well.'

Time Bandits 2

Terry Gilliam has also worked on a screenplay for the long-awaited *Time Bandits 2* with another of his regular collaborators, Charles McKeown. At the time of writing, the film was held up due to a legal issue over rights to the film, but Gilliam hopes to see it in production in plenty of time to exploit its millennium-based storyline. He has decided to only produce the project, handing the directorial reigns over to David Garfath, the camera operator on the original film.

'The cast members that are alive are back – Dave's gone, Jack's gone and Tiny's gone. But we do have Jack's daughter. We're gonna have girl time bandits this time, and the old ones are a bunch of alkies sitting on the edge of heaven, drinking meths and talking about the good old days. The child is a girl this time, a girl who's into computers and the web. It's an odd one to go back to. I think we've got enough funny stuff in there, but there's this slight feeling of repetition in how you deal with time. I know that we made a really, really good film and any follow up is never as good. They never are.'

Attractions

Don Quixote

Gilliam and McKeown also collaborated on several drafts of a screenplay based on the tale of Don Quixote. 'I was in one of my post-film depressions: PMS – Post *Munchausen* Syndrome,' recalls Gilliam, 'And I was getting frustrated because several things weren't coming together on several fronts. I called Jake Eberts up, who had been the executive producer on *Munchausen*, and I said, "I need $20 million and I've got two names for you – one's Quixote, one's Gilliam." He said "Done". And then I sat down and read the book, and it took me a couple of weeks to read it and it was like, "fuck, what have I said?" The book just overwhelmed me and I thought, "Jesus what do I do?" So Charles and I started working away on it. I location-scouted in Spain, post Ridley Scott's *1492*. I went down after Ridley and sort of followed his trail in some ways. Ridley's got a good eye, so we ended up looking at the same places.'

The director remains uncertain of the project's future, however, obviously feeling that the Baron in *Munchausen* and Parry in *Fisher King* have already plundered the character of Quixote to a degree. 'I think one of the reasons I've resisted it is because it keeps ending up being *Munchausen*, and Parry is definitely Quixotic. But I do think it's familiar territory, and I could be dangerously repetitive if I'm not careful. The thing I was intrigued about was it could be my Western – outside, lots of sun and horses.'

After the release of *Fear and Loathing*, Gilliam resurrected this project, this time with Tony Grisoni as co-writer, under the title of *The Man Who Killed Don Quixote*.

Anything for Billy

Gilliam does have a real Western in the works. Following a meeting with novelist Larry McMurtry during the making of *Twelve Monkeys*, Gilliam became keen to adapt McMurtry's book, *Anything For Billy*, the tale of a dime-store novelist who decides to abandon his family life to head out and explore the West he has mythologised in his work.

'But what he's been writing about is totally fictitious. He goes there to rob trains, which is just silly, but he ends up hooking up with Billy the Kid. Billy's a really interesting character and our guy is swept along with him. On the one hand he's fantasising the West like he's written about it in his dime novels. At other times the West is more fantastical than his dime novels, while at other times it's grittier. So it's a weird little battle going on with him trying to get away from being a writer, yet he is a writer. He keeps reinventing the moments, or elevating them.' At the present time, Larry McMurtry continues to work on the screenplay.

The Defective Detective

The Defective Detective is very much the fourth part of Gilliam's fantasy trilogy, telling, as it does, the tale of a burnt-out middle-aged cop who escapes to a brilliantly conceived fantasy world – full of one-dimensional cut-out tree-scapes and newspaper forests – and who ultimately sacrifices himself to protect that world.

'This is a hero who's gone sour,' says Gilliam, 'who's been brutalised by the streets of New York. He's a guy from the Midwest who came to New York to take on the Big Apple. He's a good cop and has an early initial success. He's a hero and then life goes on and he doesn't get to be a hero again. And he gets older and more tired, and his marriage is in trouble and reaching the point where he's right on the edge of a breakdown, and then he gets caught up in a world of fantasy. The trigger is a little girl's room, a girl who's gone missing. He finds himself in this fantastical world, seemingly trying to find the little girl in this world, and having to rediscover how to be a kid again, to play, because all of his tough guy stuff doesn't work in this world.'

Gilliam co-wrote the screenplay in the early 1990s with Richard LaGravenese. 'I remember on a plane ride to promote *Fisher King*,' says LaGravenese, 'he said to me, "*Fisher King* was me coming into your world. Now let's see what you do working in my world". He spelled out the whole opening to me and the concept of the detective who early in life was a hero, and ever since then had felt impotent at having any effect on the world. He had all of the pieces down. I went away and wrote a draft, and then we worked on it together.'

Numerous ideas abandoned from earlier Gilliam scripts started to find their way into *The Defective Detective*, most notably the key fantasy sequences from *Brazil* involving the sectioning and removal of the sky, and the immense wall of filing cabinets. 'The way I approached it was that I just went through all the stuff I had thrown out of all the other films and said "I've got to use this shit", a bit of recycling, nothing wasted,' remarks Gilliam.

The Defective Detective involves a lot of familiar territory, with the notable exception that the central character, as ever a Gilliam alter-ego, does not make it to the end titles. 'That's one of the reasons it scares me to do it, because I kill myself at the end, and it's very scary to do it,' says Gilliam. 'There's a side of me that doesn't want to because my films and the making of the films become one and the same thing. It's *Munchausen* scale and it scares the shit out of me because it brings back all the nightmares of *Munchausen*. I just hope that we get it together and I'm together enough, because *Fear and Loathing* was.

In a way, a blooding, because now I'm getting more ruthless in certain areas. I don't give a shit about things. I think I've got to do *Defective Detective* because it's mine. It's the purest of all the other things.

'I'm beginning to think these films are never meant to be made. You work out on them. They're your work-outs between real films. You explore ideas and characters and things, and then the right script comes along that somebody else has written and you then incorporate the ideas that have been tried out on these other things. That's kind of what's been happening, and it's getting worrisome, because there's one side of me thinks "I've got to do one of my own things again." Then sometimes I think maybe I'm not meant to do my own things anymore, the right things just fall into my lap.

'In a way, the picture I have in my head is of an artist's studio with all these half-finished canvasses all around the place, and he keeps coming back to them a year later and saying "Oh shit, that was the wrong red".'

A Gilliam sketch for the (as yet) unmade Defective Detective

Huck Finn to Highgate:
Epilogue

AT THE END OF THE LONG AND ARDUOUS interviewing process that helped shape this book, I asked Terry Gilliam the 'Big One': looking back on his body of work, *as* a body of work, what did he make of it all, at this point in time, mere months away from the impending millennium?

SCHIZOPHRENIC CARTOON MAKING AN EXORBITANT BILL FOR ITSELF

$ 1500...!!

'This is what's so awful,' Gilliam replies. 'I can't see them, I can't think about them. I don't think of it as a body of work... but I do think it's all about somebody trying to learn how to make films. Like a perpetual film student, but without going to class. It's cutting class and learning how to make films by just making them. If anything, it's probably a pretty good autobiography... that's what it may be.

'When I saw the big Matisse show a few years back – I saw it in New York – it was just breathtaking. Here was this guy who started as a proper academic painter in a sense and just grew and went through incredibly experimental things, and then suddenly took a sort of busman's holiday, wasting time down in Cannes and Nice just painting babes, obviously having a good time, as it was really mediocre stuff. Then he was getting older and becoming almost blind and becoming almost like a child again, cutting things out of paper. And it was the most touching thing because a life was there. I would like to think the films have a fair representation of the development of somebody. Not necessarily a filmmaker, but somebody. That's what it feels like. I fear when people say to me their favourite film of mine was *Time Bandits*. I think "what about all these other ones, have I just been wasting my life?" Or if *Brazil* is the one that's going to go on my tombstone.

'I can't think of anything more frightening than being nominated for an Academy Award because I'm not sure I want the company. The company that didn't get the awards is more interesting. I think what's good about the stuff is people have strong memories of the films. They linger, and that's what I set out to do – to leave my memories in other people's brains.'

Filmography

The Cry of the Banshee (1969) — titles animator
And Now for Something Completely Different (1971) — co-writer, performer, animator
A Short History of Flight (1972, short) — director, writer, animator
Monty Python and the Holy Grail (1974) — co-director, co-writer, performer, animator
Jabberwocky (1977) — director, co-writer
Monty Python's Life of Brian (1979) — designer, co-writer, performer, animator
Time Bandits (1981) — director, writer, producer
Monty Python Live at the Hollywood Bowl (1982) — co-writer, performer
The Crimson Permanent Assurance (1983, short) — director, writer, performer
Monty Python's The Meaning of Life (1983) — co-writer, performer, animator
Brazil (1985) — director, co-writer, performer
Spies Like Us (1985) — cameo performer
The Adventures of Baron Munchausen (1988) — director, co-writer
The Fisher King (1991) — director
Twelve Monkeys (1995) — director
The Hamster Factor (1996) — performer
Fear and Loathing in Las Vegas (1998) — director, co-writer
The Dress Pattern (1998, short) — director, writer

Bibliography

Animations of Mortality by Terry Gilliam
The Battle of Brazil by Jack Mathews
Fear and Loathing in Las Vegas by Hunter S. Thompson
The First 200 Years of Monty Python by Kim 'Howard' Johnson
The Fisher King: Book of the Film by Richard LaGravenese
From Fringe to Flying Circus by Roger Wilmut
The Life of Python by George Perry
Losing the Light by Andrew Yule
Monty Python by Douglas L. McCall

Sources

AIP and Co.
American Cinematographer
American Film
American Premiere
Cinefantastique
Cinefex
Cinema
CinemaTV Today
City Limits
Comedy Review
Daily Express
Daily Mail
Daily Mirror
Daily Telegraph
Empire
Evening Standard
Film and Philosophy
Film and TV Technician
Film Comment
Film Dope
Film Quarterly
Film Review
FilmFacts
Films and Filming
Films Illustrated
Guardian

Hollywood Reporter
Interview
Monthly Film Bulletin
New Statesman
New York Times
The New Yorker
Observer
On Location
Premiere
Prevue
Radio Times
Rolling Stone
Screen International
Sight and Sound
The Spectator
Starburst
Starlog
Sunday Telegraph
Sunday Times
Sunday Times Magazine
Time
Time Out
The Times
Village Voice
Mail On Sunday
You Magazine

...JUST PUTTING SOME THOUGHTS DOWN ON PAPER...

Pictures

Except as listed below all pictures are courtesy of Mr Terry Gilliam, from his personal collection

Designed by Will Harvey for Essential Books

The author and publishers have made every reasonable effort to contact all copyright holders. Any errors that may have occurred are inadvertent and anyone who for any reason has not been contacted is invited to write to the publishers so that a full acknowledgment maybe made in subsequent editions of this work.